Dreams and
Deconstructions

Dreams and Deconstructions

Alternative theatre in Britain

Editor: Sandy Craig

AMBER LANE PRESS

Published in 1980 by
Amber Lane Press Limited
9a Newbridge Road
Ambergate
Derbyshire

ISBN 0 906399 19 X (cased)
      0 906399 20 3 (paper)

Text set in 11/13 pt Melior, printed and
bound in Great Britain at The Pitman Press, Bath

Contents

Contributors

Sandy Craig (Editor) is a freelance journalist. He has worked with 7:84, which he helped to start in 1971, and other alternative theatre companies, and was a member of the Drama Panel of the Arts Council from 1978–80.

John Ashford is currently Theatre Director at the Institute of Contemporary Arts in London. He was the founder theatre editor of *Time Out* magazine and served on the Drama Panel of the Arts Council for a number of years.

Rosalind Asquith is a freelance journalist and is currently working for the theatre section of *Time Out* magazine. A graduate of Camberwell School of Art, she has worked in community theatre and as a teacher, photographer and designer.

Colin Chambers is theatre critic of the *Morning Star* and a regular contributor to *Plays and Players* and other theatre journals. He is the author of *Other Spaces: New Theatre and the RSC* and the general editor of the International Theatre Institute's guide *Theatre London*.

Tony Coult is an actor/teacher, writer and playleader and was until recently a member of the Perspectives Theatre Company in Peterborough. He is the author of the Methuen Theatrefile *The Plays of Edward Bond*.

Steve Grant is a journalist and playwright. He is currently the theatre editor of *Time Out* magazine and was formerly assistant editor of *Plays and Players*.

Malcolm Hay is a freelance journalist and also works as a playreader for the Royal Shakespeare Company and as an assistant editor on *Theatre Quarterly*. He is co-author of two books on Edward Bond—*Edward Bond: A Companion to the Plays* and *Bond: A Study of his Plays*.

Naseem Khan is a freelance journalist and a former theatre editor of *Time Out* magazine. She wrote a column *The Other Theatre* for the *Evening Standard* for two years, was co-author of the BBC's Hindi series *Parosi*, and is the author of *The Arts Britain Ignores: The Arts of Ethnic Minorities in Britain* (sponsored by the Arts Council, The Gulbenkian Foundation and the Community Relations Commission).

Robin Thornber is northern features writer of the *Guardian* and has been writing on the subject of regional theatre since 1968.

Michelene Wandor is a poet, playwright and journalist and is currently poetry editor and theatre critic for *Time Out* magazine. Her monograph on sexual politics and theatre is in preparation.

Foreword

The reader should be forewarned: this is not an 'objective' history of those developments in British theatre over the past decade or so which can be grouped loosely under the category 'alternative theatre'. The experts in this case are partisan: most of us have been intimately involved in the developments themselves.

Besides, the considered reflection of much historical writing seems to me to separate the past from the present; history slips behind the glass like an exhibit in a museum, bearing no relation to the present, of no practical use to the future. Safe. Even assuming it to be possible, there would be no point in writing such a history of alternative theatre which was always about changing the world not reflecting it, and which is, anyway, alive and developing, neither a dead object of the past, nor a fit subject for the historical surgeon's knife.

Neither should this book be seen as giving the 'official' insider's view of alternative theatre – though it could, perhaps, be used as a bluff-your-way guide to the subject, should the pastime become fashionable. Alternative theatre is a house of many voices, most of them dissenting: this book echoes those differences.

Lastly, this book is dedicated to all those groups and individuals, named and un-named, who have made this book possible: the alternative theatre workers themselves.

Sandy Craig
May, 1980

Theatre as a weapon: Roland Muldoon and Red Saunders of CAST.

1 Reflexes of the Future

The beginnings of the fringe

Sandy Craig

"The work of art is valuable only in so far as it is vibrated by the reflexes of the future."

André Breton

The relations between art and life are complicated and sometimes surprising. Thus, John Arden has written: "A curious circumstance about the content of my plays – years after they have been written and performed, events have as it were come full circle, I find my imaginative figments turning out as established fact, by no means invariably to my satisfaction. *Serjeant Musgrave's Dance* (1959) dealt with a massacre of civilians during a British Army colonial 'peace-keeping' operation at the same time as a bitter colliery strike in England. In January 1972 thirteen people were shot dead by the Paras in Derry, while industrial trouble raged in the coalfields on a level unknown since the 1920s." [1] By the autumn of that year John McGrath had adapted Arden's original play and the 7:84 Theatre Company was touring England with *Serjeant Musgrave Dances On*. Life imitates art, and art – as cudgel of the imagination – reciprocates the gesture.

Breton's remark, however, indicates something more than either the reversal of the ancient aesthetic which states that art imitates life or that theatre necessarily contains the gift of fortune-telling. Alternative theatre almost alone amongst the arts in the past decade has identified itself with that tradition of the oppressed which teaches us that the state of emergency in which we live is not the exception but the rule. It became a social seismograph of the seventies, registering long-buried underground pressures well before they rose to the surface of social life. And, in this process of expression, it helped to bring into existence hidden, exploratory ways of feeling and perception. This process is more than just a response to 'reality', it is an attempt to create a demand which has yet to be fully satisfied.

That demand is three-fold: to restore theatre to its traditional position of importance by re-creating a fresh, unsullied language of theatre; to extend the social basis of theatre to include the working class, the oppressed and the dispossessed; and to make obvious the enjoyment and the possibility of creation – particularly, collective creation – as something neither mysterious nor the privilege of the elite few but the democratic right and the inherent human capacity of the many. That demand is still being created and because of this any assessment about the success or failure of alternative theatre is necessarily provisional.

The growing establishment tendency, a form of thinking hall-marked by the Arts Council, is to conceive of British theatre – sex comedies and murder mysteries in London's West End, Shakespeare and the classics at the National Theatre and the Royal Shakespeare Company, sex, murder and Shakespeare at the carbon-copy and gin-and-tonic rep theatres, and the altogether more explosive mixture of socialism, song, satire, community expression, twilight entropy and apocalyptic dada in the protean assembly of political, community and experimental theatre groups which make up alternative theatre – in terms of a spectral continuum shading indivisibly from the ultra-violet to the infra-red. This analysis is, however, often only an attempt by the establishment to incorporate and thus defuse potentially revolutionary initiatives.

In any case it is more accurate to see the theatrical landscape as divided, a geographical reflection of the historical development of British theatre which, since the Second World War, has undergone vast structural changes. This process of change has not been a continuous series of innumerable tiny steps, one leading to the next like beads on a rosary, each stage so nearly identical to the last that distinctions are insignificant, but a history fissured with abrupt transformations, shot through, meteor-like, with two decisive rejections of tradition. The first of these led to the subsequent development and dominance of subsidized bourgeois theatre. The second, a decade or so later, led to the development of alternative theatre, a theatre in conscious opposition to both commercial and subsidized theatre, a theatre which wished to be entertaining but not bound to the profit principle, which sought to throw off the shackles of naturalism and portray what happened without the endless speechifying of internally motivated 'characters', which depended on the dynamic of action instead of the slow-paced, boring creation of the illusion of 'real life'.

In its evolution from 'underground' to 'fringe' and 'alternative' theatre, this theatre has maintained its separation from the commercial and bourgeois theatres, though this has been achieved despite greatly increased Arts Council patronage and despite the tactic of 'strategic penetration' adopted by most of the first generation of highly talented playwrights, most notably David Hare, Howard Brenton and David Edgar. The challenge for alternative theatre has been and is, continually, to set a course between the Scylla and Charybdis of incorporation into the mainstream and cultural ghettoization.

"And when they ask us how dangerous it was, we'll never tell them." Theatre Workshop actors Brian Murphy (left) and Murray Melvin in Joan Littlewood's production of *Oh What a Lovely War* (1963).

The First Theatre Revolution

The development of the subsidized theatre and the introduction of a new generation of playwrights including Osborne, Pinter, Arden, Wesker and others stems from the 'theatrical revolution' at the Royal Court in the mid-fifties. As Kenneth Tynan put it:

> "After the launching of the English Stage Company at the Royal Court in 1956, and the revelation of John Osborne, a semblance of serious thought and a flood of non-refined feeling invaded the theatre ... Moreover, one found ... that one's social and political beliefs were being engaged and challenged in a way that English drama since Shaw's heyday had rarely attempted."[2]

The intervention of the Royal Court was complemented by the growing recognition of Joan Littlewood's Theatre Workshop at the Theatre Royal in

London's East End. In particular, her production of Brendan Behan's portrait of a prison before a hanging, *The Quare Fellow*, not only treated a burning social issue (the question of the death penalty) but also re-introduced the vernacular onto the British stage after a long absence.

A few months earlier Beckett's absurdist classic *Waiting for Godot*, which is still influential for its dismissal of conventional plot, its use of stage imagery and its borrowing of popular music-hall routines, had finally received its English premiere. A few months later Brecht's Berliner Ensemble was to visit London and demonstrate that there were positive values in actors on stage not being glamorous. This was the beginning of the slow and uneven assimilation of Brecht's ideas, in particular his ideas on acting and staging.

The subsidized theatre, however, didn't stop at changing the tone, style and content of the plays, nor even at reforming the theatrical repertoire so that the classics, particularly Shakespeare, became the cornerstone of theatre programming in fact as well as theory: the new subsidized theatre insisted on its own buildings. Since the opening of the Belgrade Theatre in Coventry in 1958 – the first theatre to be built in Britain for over thirty years – there has been a spate of municipal and university theatre building unparalleled in history.

Moreover, those theatres not only reflected the civic pride and temporary affluence of local government, they also abandoned wholescale the Italianate architecture of the nineteenth-century playhouse, which encapsulated the class divisions of capitalist society in its horseshoe-shaped strata of boxes and galleries and imposed picture-frame productions in favour of supposedly more egalitarian auditoria and more flexible staging. The ideologues of the fifties who had supposed that the post-war affluence was creating a classless society found their architectural echoes not only in the ubiquitous shopping centres of the sixties and seventies but also in these expensive, concrete culture palaces carefully set apart – whether in rubble-strewn or landscaped lots – from the turmoil of everyday life. By 1976 the subsidy revolution had received the royal approval and a hundred-year dream transformed into nightmare reality: the National Theatre opened. Architecturally this was the distillation writ large of the worst excesses of the new theatre. In the behind-stage machinery it expressed a mindless utopian belief in technology; in the auditoria it equated democracy with anonymity; and in its foyers it transmuted luxury into airport-lounge transience.

The subsidized theatre's quick growth to dominance was aided by the debility of the commercial theatre. In 1950 the West End with its nationwide touring empire still ruled the roost, presenting plays, musicals and variety shows for its audiences' entertainment, its stars' glorification and its owners' profits. Already, however, its function of entertainment was being challenged by the new mass media, which were creating their own stars, while beneath the gaudy surface the industry's structure was crippled by monopolization. By the mid-fifties 'The Group' – the consortium which controlled over fifty percent of all commercial theatres – had become desperately over-extended financially. Luckily for 'The Group', its theatres were often situated on prime development sites. It indulged in an orgy of asset-stripping and diversified into films, commercial television and other forms of entertainment.

With enemies like that, the new civic reps hardly needed friends: unfortunately, neither did they seriously bother to court the commercial theatre's audiences who turned instead to television – especially the new commercial television – bingo and other leisure pursuits. By the seventies, so the critical consensus has it, the subsidized theatre – geared to its audiences' aesthetic edification and with the artistic director rather than the producer at the helm – had become unequivocally the British theatre. But by the end of the seventies, in an increasingly harsh economic climate, those same reps which had formerly cold-shouldered the commercial theatre's audiences were employing wilder and wilder stratagems to attract them back.

In their rejection of West End show-biz aims and practices, the dominant subsidized theatre epitomized by the Royal Court emphasized not only theatre as art, as opposed to theatre as entertainment, but in addition derived their notions of art from those currently in vogue in the expanding centres of higher education. The heritage of Leavis was pervasive and the belief in the central civilizing importance of literature and the concept of a literary tradition found a ready fit with the new subsidized theatre, its espousal of literary values and its pursuit of presenting the 'classics'. The new generation of theatre men were university-educated; the audiences likewise were beneficiaries of the 1944 Education Act. Meritocracy was supposedly replacing aristocracy. While the traditional theatre-going public of the commercial theatre – the colonialist upper-middle class, the petty bourgeoisie, the debs, the demi-monde of fashion and the assorted hangers-on were in decline, theatres like the Royal Court very quickly identified and developed a new theatre-going public – the professional middle classes, the technocrats, teachers and technicians: the new middle class. (It is no accident that *Look Back in Anger*, which so perfectly embodied this new audience's hopes and frustrations, was the torch that set the theatre alight. In its emphasis on the regional over the metropolitan, in its partisan treatment of the university-educated, in – most of all – its central figure of a provincial graduate who runs a sweet-stall (and thus, incidentally, neither classless nor working class as contemporary myth had it), reads the heavy Sunday papers and specializes in tirades against the injustice of the world and the 'system', *Look Back in Anger* projects a model of the world both excitingly new and deeply familiar to that audience.)

The central and differentiating element of the bourgeois subsidized theatre was that it established the primacy of the text: the production merely unchained the imprisoned life of the play-script. Unlike the commercial theatre, which called itself 'show *business*' and which frequently and narcissistically portrayed itself (as in the sentimental chorus-girl to star genre), the new subsidized theatre mystified the production process. This mystification went hand in hand with other changes: with, paradoxically, the growing importance of the director and the fetishization of the text. The structure of theatre was mis-perceived, just as society was mis-perceived, as apparently classless and with everyone pulling together. Additionally, naturalism, the dominant form of bourgeois theatre contained political argument: any such arguments were merely the expressions of individual characters usually, and ideally, held in check by the counter-arguments of other characters. In this the theatrical form echoes the political form, the checks and balances inbuilt into the parliamentary process. The fact that dramatic conflict is homologous to political consensus helps to explain why, though some plays genuinely expressed facets of class tensions, the naturalistic theatre serves only to defuse any audience action outside the building – a process aided by purging, in true Aristotelian fashion, the audience of any anti-social emotions and reducing them to a mass of passivity.

British theatre was hardly further on from the situation depicted in Chekhov's prophetic remark in his letter to Suvorin:

> "But what about us? We depict life as it is, but we refuse to go a step further. We have neither near nor remote aims and our souls are as flat and bare as a billiard table. We have no politics and we do not believe in revolution . . . But he who wants nothing, hopes for nothing and fears nothing cannot be an artist." [3]

The Moment of 1968.   The theatrical revolution inaugurated by the Royal Court can be dated exactly from a small set of productions. But alternative theatre did not start from a single seed, and though for many it quickly assumed the cultural equivalence of warfare it wasn't, unlike wars, declared on one particular day. One year does, however, stand out. As Peter Ansorge, perhaps the earliest historian of alternative theatre, insists: "It is impossible to deny, for instance, a link between the most publicized political events of 1968 and the creation, in practical terms, of the new 'alternative' circuit of arts labs, cellar theatres and environmental venues . . . Unquestionably, 1968 was the watershed." [4]

The 'most publicized' political events of '68 include the May revolt of students and workers in France; the police riot at the Democratic Convention in Chicago; the Prague Spring and the brutal Russian invasion of Czechoslovakia that followed. There were continuing race riots and student sit-ins in America and the massacre at the Mexico Olympic

Games. There was the escalating war in Vietnam and, following the banning of a Civil Rights March in Derry, the beginning of the war in the North of Ireland. Across the world, large-scale, revolutionary demands by students, workers and peasants were answered by massive and brutal repression ordered by governments of every political leaning – capitalist, communist or social-democratic. And every tear-gas grenade exploding, every policeman's boot kicking, every Buddhist priest burning was voyeuristically filmed, as it was happening, for television.

In 1968, as now, the world overflowed with milk and honey, yet the majority of its inhabitants were starving. Economically, the world's unrivalled prosperity led to demands for the equal distribution of the world's wealth. Ideologically, the possibility of material freedom was complemented by demands for cultural and creative freedom: one of the most significant calls from the barricades of Paris was for "power to the imagination".

In Britain there was no shortage of people ready to answer that call to arms. 'Underground' theatre groups blossomed into existence by the score. In London: Portable Theatre, the Pip Simmons Group, Incubus, the Wherehouse/La Mama Company, Ed Berman's Inter-Action with its lunchtime theatre off-shoot the Ambiance Lunch Hour Theatre Club, its children's theatre section Dogg's Troupe and its (slightly later) experimental company TOC, the Agitprop Street Players (later to become Red Ladder) and Freehold. In Brighton: the Brighton Combination. In Bradford: Albert Hunt's Bradford College of Art Group. In Leeds: John Fox's Welfare State. And in Edinburgh, at the beginning of 1969, the Traverse Theatre Workshop directed by Max Stafford-Clark.

By the beginning of the seventies the infrastructure for this new theatre had been created. In 1968, though the critics never noticed, new venues were opening everywhere to host the work of the groups: the Arts Lab in Drury Lane, the Theatre Upstairs at the Royal Court, the Open Space Theatre under Charles Marowitz in Tottenham Court Road and the ICA under Michael Kustow at the Mall. Others round the country quickly followed.

It is easy, however, to over-emphasize the importance of these venues. In retrospect, the ventures at the Open Space and the ICA are more representative as the final flings of a European tradition of the avant-garde than as the first gestures of a full-blooded radical alternative. While at the Royal Court, artistic director William Gaskill has stated that his motives for opening the Theatre Upstairs were two-fold: to present new work faster and cheaper, and to provide a bridge between traditional and experimental theatre.[5] Neither aim was radically new, while the latter can be seen as a way of siphoning off talent and incorporating oppositional elements into the mainstream.

But the largest claims have always been made for Jim Haynes' short-lived Arts Lab, the mecca of the underground society and a centre for cultural – and chemical – experiment. Here there were none of the hampering restrictions of traditional theatre. Indeed, Haynes positively valued the new and experimental, both stylistic and technological. Furthermore, the Arts Lab had a ready-made fairly homogeneous audience, an audience that had no preconceptions about what theatre should be, a willingness to enjoy the rough – indeed, to equate technical shortcomings with their own counter-culture – a delight for the strange, the bizarre and the physically adventurous and an appetite for ever-changing cultural sensation. The Arts Lab was the performing focus for a number of the new groups including Pip Simmons, Portable, Freehold and the earlier-established People Show. It also became the model for the mushrooming nationwide network of arts labs and counter-cultural venues such as the York Arts Centre and the St George's Project in Liverpool.

In turn, the groups – particularly Portable – were instrumental in establishing this network. Within three years the combination of an existing network of venues complete with partisan audiences, the groups' own anti-metropolitan bias and sometimes romantic attachment to the nomadic life, the almost complete lack of coverage in the traditional media (media attention always focuses cultural activity on London) and a cheap, ubiquitous form of transport in the Ford Transit and similar vans helped establish touring as the organizational model for alternative theatre. This pattern remained substantially unmodified for almost five years until, with the defection of some of the major 'fringe' writers (notably, Brenton and Hare) to more traditional venues, with the growing importance of the London fringe theatres and with the 'professionalization' of alternative theatre, activities began to centre once again in London.

In addition to the speedy establishment of an infrastructure, three other developments of 1968 aided the emergence of, and were to have a lasting effect on, alternative theatre. Firstly, the magazine *Time Out* began publication, providing an information service about the groups' activities and productions – always from a supportive, partisan position. This was of invaluable aid when the rest of the media either ignored or sneered at the groups. Secondly, the Arts Council set up a sub-committee (which later became the New Activities Committee) to investigate these new theatrical happenings: within a year it found itself subsidizing alternative theatre. Though for 1969/70 this was a miserly £15,000, this was to be the beginning of continuing and increasing support for alternative theatre. (The groups themselves were for years divided about the desirability of depending on state funding – a problem I will return to in the final chapter.) Lastly, in September '68, the Theatres Act was passed and the Lord Chamberlain's function as pre-censor of theatre officially ceased. Where for centuries playwrights had had their work hacked about by the 'royal smut-hound', alternative theatre from the moment it breathed life was under no such restrictions. Whether the groups would have paid any attention to the restrictions had they been in force, whether they would even have bothered to notify the Lord Chamberlain, is open to doubt – as is the ability of the police, already reeling from the pursuit of 'pot', to have tracked down the offenders in the already labyrinthine underground.

However, this aesthetic freedom, while allowing unprecedented experiment, may also have led both to a naivety in the groups' view of the 'system' and, paradoxically, to a cruelty in performance, a cruelty expressed either in attempts to shock for shock's sake or in 'fascistic' audience participation. In turn, the speedy realization first that the shocking wasn't shocking the right people, i.e. the bourgeoisie, because the plays were being performed to the cultural ghetto of the alternative society, and second that the stage could so obviously exert its power over the audience that was there, may be seen, transmuted, in many of the themes and obsessions of the early underground playwrights: violence, power, sado-masochism and paranoia. In some cases at least, freedom was gained but responsibility was denied.

It is sometimes thought that the best conditions for art are those which impose boundaries, that total aesthetic freedom leads only to decadence and self-indulgence. In part this may be true; but though the early groups had total aesthetic freedom there was one important limiting factor which acted as a useful creative lubricant: lack of money. Financial restrictions, underpinned ideologically by a revolt against the materialist values of capitalism, imposed an economy of means on the productions, proscribing the use of cumbersome stage technology and detailed, expensive naturalistic sets.

The strategy of the emergent alternative theatre can be contrasted with that of Marowitz at the Open Space which, despite sporadic successes, has never had a coherent policy. Marowitz, a popularizer of avant-garde techniques for middle-brow audiences (his own self-description), has explained this lack of coherence as a necessary consequence of lack of funds. However, this is disingenuous. The failure of the Open Space is not a shortage of money – other groups, for instance Pip Simmons, have maintained a coherent and exciting artistic policy on a shoe-string – but the failure of Marowitz himself to perceive that his model of experimental theatre based on the hugely subsidized laboratory situation enjoyed by Grotowski or Brook was unattainable in Britain. This should not be taken to imply that the best art is necessarily produced in garrets, but only that, in the historical situation of the recent past, the groups' strategy of making a virtue out of the necessity of limited resources was the correct one, while Marowitz's opposing strategy was not.

The result is that, while Marowitz's theatrical experimentalism has never taken root, the past decade has brought forth a profusion of alternative theatre groups. These groups are still marked, and their differences in part explained, by the profusion of influences on alternative theatre: the energy and popularity of rock music; the speed and narrative strength of the film; the striking visual insights and social spoofery of Dada and the tradition of modern art from surrealism and Kurt Schwitters to Pop Art and Happenings; and, most of all, the audiences which came from the diverse 'youth movement', a movement which encompassed the hippies and the international situationists, a confusion of esoteric religious sects and student politics, alternative psychiatry and drugs; a movement which espoused the mutually contradictory strategies of operating an autonomous alternative society within the bowels of capitalist society, of 'doing your own thing', and of community action.

The groups' ideologies were, similarly, as diverse, united only in the fact of opposition to the 'system', to those who dictated taste and to the conventional theatre.

Harbingers of the Storm

A myopic concentration on one year, 1968, distorts the emergence of alternative theatre by excluding a part of history: the tradition of oppositional politics which extends from the 'old' New Left through CND to the Vietnam Solidarity Campaign. Such a concentration emphasizes the anarchistic anti-politics stance at the expense of the tradition of Marxist socialism; it focuses attention on May '68 in Paris at the expense of the imperialist war in Vietnam; and, by implying that the class composition of the early underground theatre was exclusively student and middle-class drop-outs, it ignores the crucial minority of working class theatre workers.

Perhaps more importantly, the parallel assumption that the underground groups weren't influenced at all by previous theatre ignores a number of previous projects which sought to re-define theatre. 1968 was in many respects lift-off year for alternative theatre but, like all earthquakes, it was preceded by a number of warning tremors.

The first of these can be dated as far back as 1960 when it became obvious to at least two of our foremost playwrights that though the 'Royal Court revolution' had changed the content of plays, the Janus problem of the context of theatre and the audiences for theatre remained untouched. The two playwrights were Arnold Wesker and John Arden (with Margaretta D'Arcy).

Wesker attempted to tackle the latter problem by proposing a national network of people's theatres organized through the Labour movement. But despite years of organizing and an initially large trade union response, Centre 42 (named after the 1962 TUC resolution proposing support for the Arts) never succeeded in attracting the public in any numbers. It was donated the Roundhouse, but by the time that was opened (again, in 1968), Centre 42 had been dissolved. Wesker had wished to make theatre available to everyone without imposing establishment culture on them.

But in seeking to enrich the lives of the working class, he had imposed his own cultural values on them. And had been rejected.

Where Wesker sought to organize people to go to the theatre, Arden and D'Arcy attempted to take theatre to the people; where Wesker's attempt was national, Arden and D'Arcy's continuing attempts were local and community-based. From 1960, with their production of *The Business of Good Government*, the Ardens have been early pioneers of community and children's theatre working in Kirbymoorside and the Beaford Centre in Devon. By 1968 they were working with Ed Berman at Inter-Action's Ambiance Lunch Hour Theatre Club, with CAST at the revitalized Unity Theatre and with the ICA. Alone amongst the fifties generation of playwrights, Arden has identified himself with, and chosen to work within, alternative theatre: the theatrical establishment has rewarded him accordingly with ostracization and critical castigation. (Very few of the older playwrights, no matter how angry and radical, have sought to work even sporadically in alternative theatre. The only exception is Edward Bond who has written occasional pieces for the Anti-Apartheid Movement, CND, Gay Sweatshop, the Almost Free and the Royal Court's Young Activists Club.)

By 1963 the practical enquiry into the foundations of theatre was extended by the opening of The Traverse Theatre in Edinburgh (by Jim Haynes). This continued the function of the old London theatre clubs in presenting new plays and new writers. However, it changed the milieu from that of the aesthete to that of the disaffiliated, whether beatnik or CND supporter. In the same year, publisher John Calder staged the first nude 'Happening' at the Edinburgh Festival Fringe. This was the first realization in Britain of the concept of the 'Happening' and helped to introduce the ideas of artists like Jean-Jacques Lebel who sought to demolish the gap between life and art. Lebel's practice was the theatrical equivalent of the international situationist's political theory of the spectacle of every-day life which, in a revision of Marx, stated that the focus of capitalist domination was at the point of consumption, not the point of production. The influence of Lebel and the international situationists was widespread – from performance art groups and writers like Howard Brenton and Snoo Wilson to more authentic Marxists like John McGrath.

Calder's 'Happening' and the establishment of the Traverse reflected the growing importance of the Edinburgh Festival Fringe as a centre for experiment. In the early sixties it had hosted *Beyond the Fringe* and helped boost the satire wave. By the mid-sixties, through the example of scores of companies performing in halls all over Edinburgh, it had established a new model of theatre organization. Theatre now no longer had to take place in an exclusive, designated theatre building organized hierarchically by outside managements and presented by professionals. The new patterns of organization developed by ad-hoc companies for the three weeks of the Edinburgh Festival were to become the organizational models for most alternative theatre companies, while, after 1968, the Edinburgh Festival Fringe became one of the most important shop-windows for the groups.

Meanwhile, in London, Brook and Marowitz launched their 'Theatre of Cruelty' season for the Royal Shakespeare Company in 1963/64. This explored the ideas of Artaud and culminated in the production of Peter Weiss's *Marat/Sade*, which pitched the political and psychological head-long against each other to great effect. Two years later, working with Albert Hunt and Adrian Mitchell, Brook produced *US* for the RSC – a group-written and improvised documentary polemic on the American involvement in Vietnam.

Outside London the early sixties showed that, while the 'Royal Court revolution' had failed, the new subsidized rep system it had helped to establish was not monolithic. Peter Cheeseman at the Victoria Theatre in Stoke-on-Trent, Terry Hands at the Liverpool Everyman Theatre and Alan Plater at Hull Arts Centre were all, in different ways, trying to integrate their theatres into the community.

Lastly, there were other less easily categorizable theatrical influences: the anarchic comedy of Bruce Lacey and the Alberts with their *An Evening of British Rubbish*; the success of Joan Littlewood's *Oh What a Lovely War*; and the visits of the American Living Theatre in 1964, the La Mama and Open Theatre Companies' visits in 1967 and the first production of Jerome Savary's continental group in that same year. However, more influential than all these was the formation in 1965 of two, very different, companies whose work may truly be described as seminal: the People Show and CAST (Cartoon Archetypical Slogan Theatre), both of which are still prospering and developing.

Categorizing the Uncategorizable

Alternative theatre resists easy categorization. The boundaries between different areas remain unclear and shifting. Individual groups often start out as one thing and end up as something different. Nevertheless, the broad lines of development within alternative theatre were established early on and groups, then and now, can be differentiated into categories: (1) political theatre companies; (2) community theatre; (3) groups exploring the area between theatre and education; (4) performance art groups; and (5) companies who – whether they wished to change the production process or emphasize the visual, as opposed to the verbal, elements of performance – adopted the traditional role of theatre: presenting plays.

The importance of each area has, of course, fluctuated over the years. Political theatre, for instance, has increased dramatically in influence and has subdivided into socialist, feminist and gay sections, while lunchtime theatre now looks like a phenomenon of the early seventies.

Political theatre. Roland Muldoon and Claire Burnley formed CAST, which was to foreshadow so many later developments, after they had been kicked out of the Communist Party-dominated Unity Theatre where they had been trying to increase its popularity. They began working in pubs and folk-clubs as a conscious rejection of theatre. There they developed a stylistic mix of physical characterization, cartoon signification and a quick-cutting narrative technique (thus, cartoon archetypes) which have more in common with cinema techniques than the 'agitprop' of the twenties and thirties. Their shows maintained the machine-gun pace of the Hollywood thriller but this suspense was sustained through the conflict of political ideas, ideas usually illuminated by the ideologically unsound fumblings of CAST's central character, Muggins, a working-class Everyman caught in the switchback of history. CAST's success lay in making the audience identify with Muggins in such a way that they recognized Muggins' problems and mistakes as their own.

From the beginning, political theatre has had to run the dilemma between not selling out on the one hand and being marginalized on the other, a dilemma which is sometimes resolved into a conflict between 'the popular' and 'the political'. One person has, however, successfully evaded this conflict: Ken Campbell. Campbell has been very influential throughout alternative theatre. His early Road Shows opened up a pub circuit and

A noted feature of the Ken Campbell Road Shows was their scurrilously scatalogical concern for poking objects up people's orifices. Sylveste McCoy is the long-suffering performer.

were the forerunners of a form of pub theatre best exemplified nowadays by the Covent Garden Community Theatre (who, however, usually base their shows around some community or political issue). In its presentation of a variety mix of dramatized bar-room tales, stunts (escapology, ferrets down trousers and so on) and hard-edged, often cruel comedy, Campbell's Road Show struck a deliberately populist stance. The formula was successful but short-lived and Campbell has developed his unique brand of zany comedy and fantasy into more theatrical form with the Science Fiction Theatre of Liverpool. (Significantly, the other split-off from the Road Show was the socialist theatre company Belt & Braces which tackled head-on the popular/political dilemma that had always been latent in the Road Show.) Meanwhile, Campbell's attachment to comedy, stunts and the larger-than-life — his shows, e.g. *Illuminatus* and *The Warp* are often of epic proportions — places him in the long-standing populist entertainment tradition which had its heyday in the northern commercial theatres earlier this century.

Community theatre.   The problem of popularity has been resolved by community theatre by situating the concept of 'popularity' in the context of a particular locality and by seeking to become central, as opposed to peripheral, in the network of relations within that locality. (Locality should be understood not only in a geographical sense but also demographically.) This sense of popularity is, of course, totally opposed to that developed by the mass media which assess popularity in terms of stardom and ratings, and which is characterized by the one-way devouring attention of the fans — a psychopathic emotion that fetishizes the object of affection while simultaneously undermining the self-image of the fan. The typical result is passivity interspersed with random bursts of anarchic destructiveness: the exactly opposite effect from that intended by community theatre, which seeks to improve the self-image of its audiences.

Community theatre is often closely associated with political theatre, and distinctions often have to remain provisional. For instance, the Half Moon (in London's East End) is perhaps better seen as a political theatre operating within a particular locality, while the Albany in Deptford is a community theatre much involved in political campaigns, e.g. Rock Against Racism. This difference is partly explained by the different ambiance of the theatres — the Combination's shows at the Albany are presented in a cabaret atmosphere as part of an evening's entertainment, while the Half Moon is a fairly typical 'art' theatre; and partly explained by reference to the other activities of the organization. The Albany offers a wide range of cultural presentations and community activities, while the Half Moon restricts itself to traditional theatre activities (though these include its own Youth Theatre Team) and its foyer contains exhibitions organized by the Half Moon Photographic Gallery, one of the leading political photographers' groups in the country.

But the difference between political and community theatre ultimately lies in the differing perception of the social function of theatre: whether theatre is seen as a weapon or as community expression. Even these ideas overlap, as the case of the Combination aptly illustrates.

Originally set up in Brighton (and called the Brighton Combination) as a theatre restaurant producing straight fringe plays, particularly those of Howard Brenton and John Grillo, the Combination abandoned its Brighton premises in 1970 and for a year toured the country presenting *The NAB Show*, a show about social security. The show and the tour were organized in conjunction with the emerging Claimants' Union, and the company stayed behind after each performance to help organize or strengthen local branches of the Union. Indeed, the claim has been made on their behalf that they were the driving force behind the early successes of the Claimants' Union. Whether exaggerated or not, the Combination certainly fulfilled – in a manner which few later political groups have done – the central function of agitprop: agitate, educate and organize. However, from the beginning of 1972 they ceased touring, settled at the Albany, Deptford and became involved with the local community and its grass-roots political and social organizations.

The most influential model for community theatre, however, has been Ed Berman's Inter-Action, in North London (and, in the past few years, also in Milton Keynes). Inter-Action is, in fact, an umbrella organization involved in a wide range of community and self-help projects as well as the presentation of professional theatre of a number of different types. These latter have included Dogg's Troupe, a children's theatre company which toured the housing estates of the local community presenting participatory drama in the form of Game Plays; an environmental theatre project, the Fun Art Bus, a double-decker bus with theatre and video-screening and actors performing from the boarding deck to bus-queues; and TOC (The Other Company) which, under Naftali Yavin, examined sociological theories of role-playing and game theory in an attempt to break through the artificial barriers which exist not only between people but also between stage and audience.

Berman also helped create the Ambiance Lunch Hour Theatre Club and the Almost Free Theatre. Unlike other lunchtime theatres, which were too often merely showcases for writers or actors operating within the mixed-market theatre economy of London, these sought to subvert the practice of theatre-going as a paying evening leisure activity patronized by an elite self-regarding 'theatre-going' public. The Almost Free, almost single-handedly, has transformed the idea of community from that of a geo-graphical area to that of a minority grouping with a community of interests within society. As such, it has been instrumental, with seasons of Women's Theatre and Gay Theatre, in catalysing the growth of these areas.

Theatre and education.   Widespread changes in education, the emergence of a new higher-educated middle class, a growing focus on education generally and the large-scale increase in school drama teaching (often seen as the panacea for all childhood and adolescent development problems), together with the disaffiliation of students who challenged the gap they found between their aspirations and reality, were the necessary conditions for the development from 1966 of professional Theatre-in-Education companies and amateur Youth Theatre groups. These companies presented participatory and 'developmental' drama which sought to strengthen the child's self-expression or to develop his/her critical understanding of the world. This work was spearheaded by Bill Martin's Contemporary Theatre whose *Events* was the first expression of the experience of the juvenile delinquent told from the delinquent's point of view.

Performance art.   Performance art companies are rooted as much in the visual arts as in theatre. Thus The People Show, the earliest and still the most influential performance art group, illustrates the thesis that the crucial relation for the artist is that between himself as artist and his means of expression. The performance artist is his own means of expression and The People Show's shows chart the fluctuating tensions in this relationship. Put another way, the people on stage in The People Show do not act like actors in a naturalistic play nor do they perform like popular entertainers though they sometimes emulate these techniques within the collage of atmospheres they are creating.

Walter Benjamin has noted that art of the past possessed, because of its unique individuality, an *aura*. This is no longer possible because of the modern means of mechanical reproduction. However, The People Show have avoided the pincer movement of photography and prints, and the art commodity market (which replaces aura with the fake guarantee of inflated price) which together seek to crush the visual arts. They have escaped by developing their art into the fourth dimension of time and by replacing the individual's contemplation of the art-object with the collective experience of shared perception of the art-object. But to do this it was necessary to escape from the art gallery to the theatre.

The experience of performance art is very different from the experience of theatre precisely because the relationship between stage and audience has been radically altered on both sides. Critics, floundering in search of a description, have pointed out that The People Show's shows are structured around a collage of atmospheres rather than narrative or character. They have failed to perceive that the quality of the collage and the over-riding mood evoked depends not only on the multi-media of taped sounds, music, lighting and visual stage images but also, and more importantly, on the double change effected in the stage/audience relation. Typically, the mood evoked – and not only by The People Show – is a nostalgia for the lost aura and the lost innocence of art, while, homologously, the dream-like progression of events pulls the audience psychologically into the lost past of the subconscious.

The Welfare State stands at the opposite end of the performance art spectrum to The People Show though they are also within that current in modern art encapsulated by the 'Happening': their leading figure, John Fox is quoted as saying, "We fuse fine art, theatre and life-style but we aim to make such categories and role definitions in themselves obsolete".[6] The Welfare State has concentrated on redefining the nature of the theatrical environment, and their backgrounds have included bridges, motorways, housing estates, the sea. Using rock music, pagan ritual, written text, but most importantly carefully structured visual images, the central element of their work has been the disparity between the theatrically-created image and the surrounding social reality. This has given their best work a sense of occasion otherwise notably lacking in all modern theatre – except at the class-ridden ritual of West End first-nighting or at those rare productions in the bourgeois theatre when the star actor performs 'dangerously'.

As Albert Hunt has said of their work:

> "The Welfare State exists to create images in the most unexpected places: in streets, on housing estates, on recreation grounds. A labyrinth made out of junk is sprayed by the fire brigade with white foam and turns into a frozen winter palace. A burning coracle is thrown into a grey canal. In the drabbest of social situations, the Welfare State plays out the role of permanent Lords of Misrule."[7]

Companies presenting plays.   This development of alternative theatre is perhaps best described as 'fringe' since the work of these companies, for all their experimentation, is recognizably theatrical. This category is normally divided into two sub-groups: actor-based companies and writer-based companies. The former, in particular, describes a bewildering variety of companies though, with different emphasis, all aim to restore the actor to his/her central position in the creation of theatre. This is achieved by laying greater stress on the non-literary means of expression such as mime, gesture, movement, masks and the stage-image. However, nearly all these companies have been dominated by a single personality, usually the director, e.g. Nancy Meckler with The Freehold, Steven Berkoff with the London Theatre Group, Mike Bradwell with Hull Truck.

Two major fringe companies resist such characterization. The first of these was the Bradford College of Art Theatre Group led by Albert Hunt. Hunt, a radical educationalist and an experimenter with Brook on US, was concerned educationally not just or even primarily with matters of the curriculum but with *how* subjects were taught. He was concerned with the relation, often inhibiting, between educational institutions and their practices, and the learning situation (involving teacher, student and material of knowledge). As early as 1967, with the help of John Fox and other visual artists, he had staged the Russian Revolution on the streets of Bradford – an exercise involving over 300 students. From this Happening-based event and other educational projects, Hunt evolved a style of working through improvisation, forming shows around striking individual theatrical images. These acted as stage metaphors for the plays' subjects and were often graphically described in their titles, e.g. *John Ford's Cuban Missile Crisis*, and *James Harold Wilson sinks the Bismarck*. These not only drew from the conventions of the popular media but satirically deflated the pretensions of the world's rulers by re-interpreting their actions as those of cinema stars acting out parts. (Bradford was for many years a centre of alternative theatre activity with Hunt at the College of Art, the director Chris Parr presenting plays by Brenton and others at the University, the political theatre group The General Will, and a number of performance artists based loosely around John Fox.)

One of the credos of the Bradford College of Art Theatre Group holds true across large sections of alternative theatre: "Always, to us, theatre arose from contradiction – between what you said you were doing, and what you were actually doing, between what people saw, and what they were told they were seeing, between the real performer, physically *there*, and the parts he said he was playing." [8] This is echoed, at a deeper level of political sophistication by Roland Muldoon of CAST: "What CAST actually did was enter dialectic into the theatre. The theory versus the practice in *Horatio Muggins*, or the social democratic analysis of peace in Vietnam against the reality of imperialism." (in *John D Muggins is Dead*).[9]

The general statement is true of the second major fringe company, the Pip Simmons Group. Though Simmons' first show was an adaptation of Jean Tardieu's *Underground Lover* and *Conversation Sinfonietta*, which typically portrayed an absurdist distrust of language, he quickly fastened onto American archetypes in shows such as *Superman* and *Do It!* and exploited a much wider range of techniques including rock music, grotesque vaudeville and the technology of dry-ice-and-strobe-lighting. Half-way between fantastic re-creation and crisis documentary, *Do It!* was based upon the activities of the American Yippies and was notable for the dichotomy between the group as characters offending the audience and the group as members of Pip Simmons clearly critical of Yippie values.

Their 1975 production, *An Die Musik*, examined the relation between representation and reality in another way. Originally presented in the Mickery Theatre, Amsterdam, *An Die Musik* was about the Nazi genocide of the Jews. The first half was an extraordinary operetta in which the company mimed *The Dream of Anne Frank*. In the second half a line of bedraggled, sentimentalized Jews in a concentration camp are forced to go through meaningless routines and games by a sadistic guard culminating in a concert recital of German classical music. By moving from dream to reality and by placing the audience in the same position as the guard,

Simmons deliberately emphasized the voyeuristic way we regard the tragedies of history: our attitude of pity for the victims of the past serves only to mask our fundamental acceptance of the necessity of history. Simultaneously, Simmons inculpates art which can, no longer, be considered 'civilizing'.

There are, of course, obvious traps in attempting theatrically to explore the voyeuristic relations between consumer and product in 'the society of the spectacle'. The danger is that the multi-layered reality of the stage presentation and the active creativity of the audience will be subverted and a monolithic image and a fetishistic audience/stage relation substituted. Indeed, this was precisely the trap that another early group, Portable Theatre, fell into in the group-written creation *Lay By*, a sensational and prurient dramatization of the world of pornography. Portable Theatre was one of the few genuine writer-based companies and was very influential until 1973 when the actors took over the company, and the writers – in particular Howard Brenton and David Hare – decamped to larger theatres.

Enforced music-making in a Nazi concentration camp in a scene from *An Die Musik*, presented by the Pip Simmons Group in 1975 at the ICA.

A Question of Style

> "Cartoons were once the exponents of fantasy as opposed to rational-
> ism. They ensured that justice was done to the creatures and objects
> they electrified, by giving the maimed specimens a second life."
> *Adorno & Horkheimer.*[10]

Despite all the differences of content, form and context, despite the
different ideologies (whether socialist, anarchist, feminist or social-
democratic), despite the different theories about the function of their art
(theatre as individual expression, theatre as weapon, theatre as community expression, theatre as dialectical mirror) – despite these many, fundamental differences there appears to be one quality shared. That quality
is to be found in the new relation between the stage and the audience, a
relation of engagement.

A clue to the meaning of this can be found in a disparaging epithet of the
establishment: the claim that this new theatre is 'cartoon' theatre, implying that it is superficial, brutal and one-dimensional. Cartoons were
originally a narrative form of visual art and certainly alternative theatre,
whether agitprop or performance art, is cartoon theatre in the sense that its
narrative style is imbued with a visual consciousness. However, the
metaphor can be extended. Theatre naturalism is like a Constable painting, complete and detailed, and forcing on its audience – composed
ideally of separate individuals – an attitude of reflection and contemplation, a contemplation of its details, its wholeness, its uniqueness. On the
other hand, cartoons emphasize the movement contained within them and
the breaks between them. Similarly, alternative theatre emphasizes action
and the breaks, or commentary, between the action: the songs, jokes,
slogans, direct reportage, the changing stance to the audience and the gap
between the signified and the signifier. In the best examples of alternative
theatre these elements, in their variety and their continuous self-reflexive
commentary, constitute a much more complex yet significantly less
mysterious form of communication than that of naturalism, which is
interested only in posing questions, not in answering them. Thus alternative theatre works when it engages the audience at the twin levels of
signifier and signified, at the level of what is being said and the way it is
being said.

Naturalism perceives the world, and its relation to the world, as one in
which 'everything connects like a never-ending Victorian novel'. There is
no doubt that the other-worldly narrator is objective, real, true. The
cartoon theatre rejects this. The homologous aesthetic theory to the
practice of naturalism is the mimetic theory, the theory that art imitates
life. The cartoon theatre also rejects this, but in its rejection splits into two
forms. Either it projects dreams or fantasies onto the audience, or it
deconstructs the world and in this process shows the audience that the
world can be changed.

The cartoons of the fantasy-theatre can easily, like dreams, have a broken logic and an obsessive Ancient Mariner grip. This was a danger the Portable playwrights ran, as one of their number, John Grillo, recognized: "To force upon the audience a guilty awareness of a darker reality beneath our smooth facades was an important objective. This was summed up for me by a young director who remarked 'The function of drama is to incriminate the audience'." [11] But a mesmeric fascination with violence could easily lead to apocalyptic anti-humanist visions sadistically imposed on an exploited audience.

However, the other category of cartoon theatre has won the day. This 'deconstructive' theatre is critical but life-enhancing, a theatre which dismantles the world in order to demonstrate the possibility of creative change, a theatre which engages the audience in a shared creativity and unplugs them from a history pulped out in head-lines and news-flashes freeing them from a reality which seeks to defeat them.

As Hans Magnus Enzensberger has noted, there is a contradiction at the heart of all the media:

> "The mind industry can take on anything, digest it, reproduce it, and pour it out. Whatever our minds can conceive of is grist to its mill; nothing will leave it unadulterated: it is capable of turning any idea into a slogan and any work of the imagination into a hit. This is its overwhelming power, yet it is also its most vulnerable spot: it thrives on a stuff which it cannot manufacture by itself. It depends on the very substance it must fear most, and must suppress what it feeds on: the creative productivity of people". [12]

But alternative theatre exults and shows its exultation in the creative productivity of people.

References

1 John Arden *To Present the Pretence* p. 155 (Eyre Methuen, 1977).
2 Kenneth Tynan *A View of the English Stage* p. 11 (Paladin, 1975).
3 Quoted by John McGrath in *Scottish International*, October 1971.
4 Peter Ansorge *Disrupting the Spectacle* p. 56 (Pitman, 1975).
5 See Terry Browne *Playwrights' Theatre* p. 84 (Pitman, 1975).
6 Quoted in Peter Ansorge *op. cit.* p. 41.
7 Albert Hunt *The Times Educational Supplement*, 25 July 1975 (quoted in an unpublished article by Clive Barker).
8 Albert Hunt *Hopes for Great Happenings* p. 103 (Eyre Methuen, 1976).
9 Roland Muldoon in an interview in *The Leveller*, April 1978.
10 Adorno, Theodor W. & Horkheimer, M. *The Dialectic of Enlightenment* pp. 121–122 (Allen Lane, 1973).
11 John Grillo *Gambit* Vol. 6 No. 23, 1973.
12 Hans Magnus Enzensberger *Raids and Reconstructions* p. 9 (Pluto Press, 1976).

2 Unmasking the Lie

Political theatre

Sandy Craig

"The lie is transformed into a world order."

Kafka.

All theatre is political in the sense that theatre is not autonomous and is forced continually to decide in whose service it acts. While most theatre-workers in the commercial and bourgeois subsidized theatres do not recognize this choice, workers in political theatre consciously place themselves on the side of the working class. Political theatre is, by necessity, a theatre of socialist political change.

Political theatre is also essentially different from the political plays that are produced in the subsidized theatre as part of a diet which includes classics, farces, murder mysteries and 'non-political' plays. It can be argued that, within the context of such a repertory and playing to the largely middle-class (and middle-aged) theatre-going public, these political plays merely illustrate the Marcusian theory of repressive tolerance. Or that the continued production but sticky critical reception of the overtly Marxist plays of the likes of Edward Bond is important mainly as an index of the extent of censorship in society or the possible rightwards drift of those establishments' artistic directors. Or, indeed, that the presentation of such plays paradoxically leads to a cultural complacency which enables, as Kafka noted, the lie to be transformed into a world order.

However, the important feature which distinguishes political plays from political theatre is this: political plays seek to appeal to, and influence, the middle class, in particular that section of the middle class which is influential in moulding 'public opinion'. The implication of this is that society can be reformed and liberalized, where necessary, by the shock troops of the middle class – and, of course, such people are influential in campaigns for reform. But, further, political plays in bourgeois theatre implicitly recognize that the middle class remains the progressive class within society. Political theatre, on the other hand, as embodied in the various political theatre companies, aims – with varying degrees of success – to appeal to, and be an expression of, the working class. Its underlying belief is that the working class is the progressive class within society.

Political theatre has grown to a position of some prominence over the past years. Indeed, the proliferation of companies can be seen as a direct consequence of the unusual set of political forces in the late sixties. However, it would be a mistake to think that the exigencies of the class struggle required or brought forth these particular companies. The class struggle may be a necessary and determining condition for the emergence of socialist theatre; but the sufficient condition for such an emergence can only be found in the will of the individuals committed to the various enterprises. It would also be a mistake to see political theatre as a completely new development created out of nothing. Of course, compared to the broad highway of 'the theatre', the history of political theatre is a twisting, dusty path – sometimes almost petering out, sometimes dividing into innumerable tracks – through out-of-the-way foothills. Nevertheless, there is a continuous presence of political theatre in Britain through the twentieth century, which can be used to illuminate the present political theatre, though it can hardly be counted as a major influence.

The Tradition of Political Theatre

Political theatre was evident as early as the nineteen-twenties with the rise of the Workers' Theatre Movement. At its height, the WTM was a national organization with over thirty member groups, its own offices and a journal, *Red Stage*, which published not only articles and news items but also scripts and songs for use by member groups. Their shows were generally short sketches, monologues and songs, organized in a revue format and performed free on the streets. The emphasis was firmly on the class struggle, not the conflict of individuals, an emphasis which was often illustrated by focusing on specific issues and performed to partisan audiences. The groups did not use props or costumes. Indeed, one group was almost expelled for using a judge's wig.

Unlike present-day political theatre companies, none of whom are formally aligned with any specific political party, the WTM was closely linked with the Communist Party (CP) and when, in the mid-thirties, the CP changed its cultural policy to the 'Popular Front' strategy – which meant among other things no attacks on potential allies like Labour politicians – and allied this to an invocation for 'socialist realism', the WTM swiftly declined. Its forte had been satiric attack, not the naturalistic mirroring of reality.

It was replaced by a more conventional form of theatre which found expression in the Unity Theatre network. These – particularly the London Unity Theatre – enjoyed a number of successes with a more international repertoire, including Clifford Odets' *Waiting for Lefty*, and productions by Brecht and O'Casey. It also developed the differing forms of the documentary play and the working class history play. These types of play, as well as the more traditional music hall, were to be taken up again by the companies in the seventies, although by the late fifties the Unity Theatre was no longer a force on the Left.

There was another development from the Workers' Theatre Movement. In 1934 Joan Littlewood and Ewan McColl had established the Manchester-based Theatre of Action in which Littlewood, who was aware of the new developments on the Continent, experimented with song, dance and expressionistic techniques. Littlewood believed that in order to change theatre radically it was necessary not merely to express political content but also to find a new theatrical form. After the war she reformed her group and founded the Theatre Workshop which toured a country-wide trade union circuit. By 1953, however, feeling that theatre could only be effective if it was based within a community, she settled the Theatre Workshop in the Theatre Royal, Stratford, in the East End of London. Here, for over a decade, she attempted to establish a popular working-class theatre.

Two Lines of Development

It is easy, however, to over-emphasize the direct influence of this tradition on the work of recent companies. The immediate descendants of Unity were CAST – but their style and politics were in direct reaction to most of the contemporary Unity productions. And though many companies have developed the use of popular song, the celebration of working-class values and the documentary format, perhaps the most immediate descendants of Joan Littlewood are to be found not in the political theatre companies but in the community groups. These groups have also developed Littlewood's ideas of a theatre aimed for a specifically local audience and giving expression to that community, and of the theatre as 'fun palace'. Meanwhile, the rest of the history of political theatre has been hidden until recently; only the ideas of Brecht can be seen to have had a widespread influence. Nevertheless, the types of theatre which, almost independently of this tradition, have been produced in the seventies, include the complete diversity of formal experimentation produced by the previous fifty years of political theatre. This in itself is no mean achievement.

Though 1968 was the watershed year for alternative theatre, the emergence of a specifically political theatre didn't occur until some two or three years later: until 1970 there was only CAST and the emerging Red Ladder. And, whereas the earlier 'underground' companies had been influenced stylistically by the visits of American and Continental theatre companies and had taken their themes from the May '68 *événements* in Paris, from student demos and the youth revolt, political theatre companies rapidly evolved their own theatrical models. These owed little to underground experimentation apart from pace, the use of music and a general concentration on image as well as words. Thematically, the political theatre took its content from its perception of working-class struggle.

The difference between the underground and the political theatre is illustrated by a reminiscence of Roland Muldoon of CAST:

> "We did a play called *The Trials of Horatio Muggins*, which was probably our best politically. In this play a worker was accused of being a bourgeois sell-out and not embracing the revolution as confused by the alternative culture people who didn't like televisions and refrigerators. He was accused of being a hard hat, a misery, a guy that had no imagination and one who justified the capitalist system. By the end of the play he turned the whole thing round and showed that they were irrelevant, that they didn't talk about the working class, and that as he'd been eating Walls sausages all his life he understood exactly what capitalism was all about.
>
> "We started to see ourselves as a mirror of the crisis of the left. Not a proper, realistic mirror but a dialectical mirror which showed all the enthusiasm of Bristol University students to lock up their vice chancellor wasn't the revolution when it came to Horatio Muggins who went to work in a factory." [1]

Chris Rawlence's description of the genesis of Red Ladder, though couched in different language, shares the same concerns:

> "Red Ladder began (in October 1968) by answering needs. The first shows were for tenants' associations in Tower Hamlets during the struggle against the GLC rent rises through 1968–69. We were asked to open meetings with sketches lasting five to ten minutes about the rent issue. The tenants wanted us to warm the meetings up, help build an atmosphere of solidarity and attract more people to the meeting." [2]

The result was a primitive, cloak-and-dagger account of the rent fight which drew on the traditions of the melodrama and the music hall.

Rejecting the inverted glamour and cult syndrome of the underground, CAST and Red Ladder developed a more authentic Marxist theatre. They showed that the primary focus of capitalist oppression is at the point of production. In this they opposed the influential analysis of the time derived from the International Situationists – and, in a different way, from the emerging Women's Liberation Movement – which saw the primary focus of oppression as operating at the point of consumption. Red Ladder began performing their next play, *Stick Your Penal Up Your Bonus*, outside the factory gates at Ford's, but found that because they had no organizational relationship with the workers there they were unsuccessful at gaining their attention: "We realized then that we had to relate to working people through their own organizations and not stay on the outside of the labour movement." [3]

The proliferation of socialist theatre companies began properly in 1970 with Bruce Birchall's West London Theatre Workshop (originally called the Notting Hill Theatre Workshop). Birchall had previously formed a company in Cambridge during his university days and had been influential in the left caucus at the yearly National Student Drama Festival. Meanwhile, in early 1971, the General Will was formed in Bradford by David Edgar, Chris Parr, Alan Hulse and others. West London, and others that were quickly to follow, worked very broadly within the agitprop tradition. The General Will tended to present panoramic documentaries of contemporary history such as *The National Interest*.

These groups were formed mainly by students or recent graduates. 7:84, formed by John McGrath in July 1971, was composed predominantly of disenchanted professional theatre workers and as such developed as a reaction to the dominant, naturalistic form of theatre rather than out of the agitprop tradition. 7:84's first play, *Trees in the Wind*, which opened on the Edinburgh Festival Fringe that year, showed both its theatrical roots (and not only in its recognizable production and acting values) and its future direction. Though performed on and around three separate stages, formally the play stuck close to naturalism in the first half only to break loose after the interval with songs and fantasy-sketches.

Within two years other companies whose roots were in theatre had formed, most notably, Foco Novo and Belt & Braces, while 7:84 itself had developed into two companies, 7:84 (England) and 7:84 (Scotland).

By the mid-seventies there were over fifteen established and permanent socialist theatre companies. There was also a consequent proliferation of styles. At one extreme there was locally-based agitprop, at the other socialist plays, often constructed along Brechtian lines. In between there were companies seeking to develop popular entertainment forms into paradigmatic models of socialist expression and other companies producing documentaries and plays which uncover working-class history. These categories refer more to individual productions than to companies who often utilize different forms for different productions. However, each individual company's strategy (and resources) is reflected in a bias towards one form of production.

This diversity of form is an important and continuing feature of socialist theatre. It is often erroneously conflated by commentators, partly from straightforward ideological reasons, partly because, with the exception of the Half Moon which has its own theatre, all these companies tour either nationally or regionally. This inevitably imposes an economy of means on the productions.

Since the mid-seventies, though there hasn't been much increase in the numbers of directly socialist theatre companies, there has been a further diversification in the development of a number of feminist theatre companies and in the emergence of Gay Sweatshop, the only *permanent* gay theatre company in Britain to date.

There is a tendency in the British left to ignore gay politics and the

Gay Sweatshop's *Mister X*, written by members of the company, Drew Griffiths and Roger Baker, on the theme of coming out as gay (1976).

issues it raises. Certainly, socialist theatre companies have rather neglected gay politics in the subject matter of their plays, though there is now much greater awareness of sexual politics in general. For this, Gay Sweatshop are partly responsible. Indeed, without their continuing presence such West End successes as Martin Sherman's *Bent* – about the Nazi persecution of gays – would have been inconceivable. Gay Sweatshop has both a men's and a women's company; it tours nationally both to the gay community, to whom it gives powerful voice, and to a wider public. Recently the men's company has sought to uncover the hidden history of gays, a project which has resulted so far in *As Time Goes By* and *For the Dear Love of Comrades*, both written by Drew Griffiths and Noel Greig. This latter production, about the life of Edward Carpenter, was remarkable in its detailing of the eventually conflicting demands, public, political and personal, on Carpenter without either reducing this complexity to simplistic contrast or in losing the basic political argument in the checks and balances of naturalistic characterization.

Meanwhile, the past five years have been a period of consolidation for the 'straight left' companies. There has been a sophistication of the existing forms and a trend towards less directly interventionist forms. This has been characterized (in my opinion wrongly) as a whole-scale switch from agitprop to naturalism. Thus, for Bruce Birchall, the history of socialist theatre is the classic case of the sell-out: "The post-1968 break-away movement became absorbed into the theatrical mainstream by state funding, and what had begun as a piece of political practice ended up as a job."[4] In reply, David Edgar criticized Birchall on the grounds that he "leaves out of account the relationship between developments within the theatre and the state of the struggle outside it."[5] For Edgar the move from agitprop towards more complex theatrical forms was a considered response by the companies to the collapse of working-class wages-militancy after 1974.

Inevitably, different political conditions will tend to call forth different forms of theatre; but this is a tendency not a necessity. Similarly, Birchall is correct in identifying a danger in state subsidy: incorporation, as I argue in the final chapter, is an ever-present and insidious lure, a strategy (unconsciously) adopted by the Arts Council to contain fringe developments. But such attempts at incorporation have only been partial: the Arts Council is not monolithic and while it entices (and not at all wholeheartedly), the critics in the press and the media consistently ignore or mis-recognize socialist theatre, and the status-endowing national companies only very warily employ its talents.

For Birchall, revolutionary theatre, which uses theatre as a weapon, is autonomous of society; for Edgar it is a direct reflection of the movement of forces within society. Both theories are stark over-simplifications of the relations between theatre and society, one tending to collapse into 'vanguardism', the other into reformism. However, in both a theoretical over-simplification is dependent on a prior historical over-simplification: both neglect the early and continuing diversity of the forms adopted by socialist theatre companies.

Preaching to the Converted

Implied in Birchall's and Edgar's interpretation of socialist theatre history as a (reactionary or progressive) switch from agitprop to naturalism is a shared mis-understanding of the function of theatre. Theatre doesn't spark off revolutions; very rarely is a performance the direct cause of riots. Socialist theatre, however, does have many different functions which are integral to the continuation of the fight for socialism: it can provide information and analysis, it can boost confidence and strengthen solidarity, it can 'raise consciousness' or, most basically, it can provide socialist entertainment. It can help re-establish the belief in socialism, it can help persuade the doubtful, it can sow seeds of doubt in the critical. It may even, on occasion, be influential in 'converting' someone to socialism: though for most socialists there was no Pauline conversion on the road to a socialist Damascus. It doesn't man the barricades or the picket lines: it raises the analysis, it puts meat on the bones of socialism.

To state that theatre causes social change or that social change changes theatre are attempts, if inadequate, to answer one of the most fundamental problems of socialist theatre: its relation to social change. This problem lies at the root of two of the commonest criticisms of political theatre. As Roland Muldoon put it:

> "The two questions which really piss me off most are: 'Aren't you preaching to the converted?' If all the people we'd ever played to were converted we'd be out winning. And the other question is: 'You don't tell us *how*.' They really want the drug, they really want the dream."[6]

Socialist theatre companies are participants in social change; but they are neither political leaders nor are they detached and objective observers looking on from the side-lines. And from the recognition that there is a shared system of beliefs between stage and audience, it does not necessarily follow that this relation is akin to that between minister and congregation. Just as the term 'agitprop' is sometimes used to conflate a variety of forms, so, homologously, the metaphor of preaching to the converted is used to define wrongly the central relationship between theatre and social change. Both become means of ignoring the different forms of participation in social change that is open to theatre.

Agitprop in fact often covers all varieties of 'tendency' theatre: street theatre, agitprop proper, issue plays, theme plays (e.g. the position of women), parable plays, working-class history plays, panoramic documentary plays, personal development plays, cabaret and revue. These, variously, use a mass of technical means: mime, movement, stylized costume and gesture, character stylization, different levels of address to the audience, monologue, aside, various types of song, intercutting of scenes, use of slogans and captions, quotes and statistics, ensemble-playing and the interruption of the action by 'acts' – magical, comic, escapological or whatever.

There are, however, two characteristics of all these forms of theatre. The first is that the content of the shows tends to present people behaving in public in reaction to public events. However, the dominant literary and theatrical tradition has assumed that the essence of individuality lies in the psychological, inner world of the individual, in his private thoughts and desires. To situate stage representations within the public world of work and the trade figures is, it is thought, to deny those representations any individuality. Indeed, such is the power of that tradition that it is difficult for writers to individualize characters other than by recourse to showing examples of their 'private' behaviour. However, to insist on the 'inner man' as the true individualization is in itself a mark of alienation.

The other characteristic is that the relation between the stage and the audience is much closer and more direct. It is more akin to the relation between the performer or entertainer and the audience than the deliberately distanced relation of naturalism, of naturalistic acting to its audience. The audience participates in the performance in the activity of its involvement. The communication is not passive but is an active creative process linking performers, productions and audience in the production of the play's meaning. Thus John McGrath has commented – about *Lay Off*, a documentary montage using music-hall, songs, variety acts and sketches to present the development of science and the rise of the multi-nationals:

> "If you're doing a show about industry and people being made redundant, about the growth of large corporations, ripping off the workers by dividing and ruling, and you're doing it for an audience which is not really involved in all that, then you find that that audience is saying, oh, what happened to *Fish in the Sea*, that lovely family story? But if you do it for an audience of people who have worked in industry, who are working in industry, then the contact is real and the dynamics of the play work through the relationship between the meaning and the audience . . . You find that people use words like 'didactic' when they're not actually involved in the meaning of it. The people who are actually involved in the meaning of it don't think of it as didactic. They think of it as self-evident . . ."[7]

The realization of the complexities involved in the relation between socialist theatre and social change – which finds concrete realization in the relationship between stage and audience – combined with the rejection of utopian hopes for instant revolution has led the companies to re-define their project, not in terms of an agitprop/naturalism dichotomy but more in terms of exploring and re-vivifying working class entertainment traditions, in entering the hidden mainstream of popular culture. From this appraisal it follows that the production of meanings in the theatre is dependent not only on the play and the play's performance (and the audience) but in the *context* of the performance.

This conclusion is by no means universally accepted by socialist theatre workers, while the very existence of a popular working-class culture is denied by the bourgeois establishment. Nevertheless, the range of initiatives taken up by the companies in the past five years can be seen as conscious or unconscious reflections of this analysis.

North West Spanner.   Superficially, North West Spanner is the archetypical agitprop group. Based since 1971 in the Manchester area they have built up carefully their own local circuit, performing in pubs, clubs and factory canteens. Their shows, which are promoted by shop stewards, trade union local organizers, and community activists, concentrate on single issues which directly affect their audiences. Thus *Winding-Up* was a show about a redundancy and fight-back at Courtaulds, while *Safety – First or Last* was about safety at work and the need for more rigorous safety standards. Short, broadly comic, with snappy, intercut scenes and presented with a minimal use of props and costumes, the play is deliberately polemical. But to see it as agitprop would be to miss much of the point. As Ernie Dalton, a member of Spanner, explained: "The *Safety* play comes from our own work experience; at a very basic level it's taking the piss out of our old work situations. And it still works. It's four years old, but it's still relevant. 'Work is bad for you' – I know, it's a joke. We're the actors in the canteen having a laugh. We are working-class theatre. That is our tradition, where our roots are, our class background."[8]

Spanner has continued in that tradition with its later play *Partisans*, which is set in the factory of a small Chrysler subsidiary at the time of the Peugeot take-over. Politically the intention was to counteract and analyse the prevailing feeling (in 1978) of cynicism and defeatism amongst trade unionists; theatrically the play was carried along by a surrealistic, anarchic comedy and an extreme caricaturization which ultimately stemmed from the Jonsonian comedy of humours. These qualities combined most notably in the eloquent visual representation of the Chairman of the Board as a three foot square white dice. (Chairman as gambler? or as tool of gamblers?)

The Manchester-based group North West Spanner with *Winding Up*, their protest play about the declining textile industry and redundancy at Courtaulds.

Red Ladder.   This is another group which, at least in its early days, was regarded as the epitome of agitprop. By 1973, however, the shows had grown longer, were more complexly organized and focused on the larger concerns of the Left rather than on single issues. Probably their most successful show of this period was *A Woman's Work is Never Done*. (This is discussed further in Chapter 3.)

By the mid-seventies, however, and with declining working-class militancy, Red Ladder felt they had to adopt a new strategy:

> "We were faced with a choice: to make a political theatre for the politically conscious sector of the working class – those who continued to be actively involved; or to seek a broad working-class audience which would be attracted to our shows first and foremost because they offered the prospect of a good night out. We opted for the latter – the building of a popular socialist theatre." [9]

This involved the group in establishing a base in Leeds and concentrating their touring in Yorkshire. Also, whereas before they'd worked through the unions, they now adopted a dual approach: they continued to produce 'labour movement' shows for the labour movement while also producing shows, like *Anybody Sweating?*, deliberately designed for and produced in clubs.

However, the experience of making *A Woman's Work is Never Done* remains crucial to their development. While their plays do not focus on sexual politics they embody a socialist-feminist perspective. This was certainly noticeable in their play about the mid-nineteenth-century Chartist movement in the industrial north, *Taking Our Time*. The play was both history play and parable play: history in its dramatization of the split between the hand-loom weavers – small producers in a chain of production – and the emergent class of wage-labourers in the mills; parable in its emphasis on the consequences of technological change and in the complex relations between economic structures and 'quality of life'. At the same time, in showing the active involvement of the women weavers, the play undermined the usual male assumption that only men make history.

Half Moon.   Red Ladder's strategy to gain a popular audience may usefully be contrasted with that of the Half Moon in London's East End. The problem the Half Moon faces is different from that of any of the other socialist theatre companies. Whereas Red Ladder choose the venues for their different shows and thereby attract specific sections of society, the Half Moon can only attract a specifically working class audience through its image as a theatre and through the biases of its programming. The Half Moon's task has not been made any easier by its geographical situation within easy distance of Fleet Street and the critics, whose acknowledgement of the merits of many of their productions has the inevitable tendency of distorting the Half Moon's original intention and turning it into an alternative – but safely alternative – Royal Court.

"And the beetles whirring like cracked bells." Woyzeck drowning in the Half Moon's visually stunning production of Georg Büchner's 1836 working-class tragedy.

   In the event the Half Moon's policy has veered between that of a socialist-inclined 'art' theatre and that of a localized community theatre with distinctively populist leanings. The most successful production exhibiting this latter trend was Shane Connaughton's Living Newspaper-styled documentary, *George Davis is Innocent OK*. In its major contribution to the successful campaign to free George Davis after a wrongful arrest and sentence, this has been an almost unique illustration of a play having a large and direct effect on society. Powerfully presented and performed to a partisan local audience, with an appeal after for contributions to help the campaign, the play's analysis of police procedure and corruption tended to be displaced by the audience's overwhelming identification with George Davis. This conspiracy between stage and audience constructed a meaning from the play which, in its suggestion that crime was a way of fighting back at capitalists and therefore capitalism, tended to endorse crime.

   Over the past three years, under the direction of Robert Walker, the Half Moon has concentrated on presenting the socialist classics of Büchner, Brecht, Toller and others. This had always been an important side to the Half Moon's policy: their early productions of *The Mother* and *St Joan of the Stockyards* have been amongst the best British productions of Brecht. The introduction of a repertoire based on the socialist classics reflects Walker's belief that the Half Moon has to, and in fact does, draw its audience as much from the middle-class socialist 'community' as from a distinctively local East End audience. It also allows him room for a much greater range of formal experimentation and his recent productions have used a wealth of expressionistic, constructivist and futuristic devices and techniques. The danger with this concern to increase 'the language of theatre' is that the ideals of popular theatre may be replaced by those of a self-centred avant-garde. It's a danger which the Half Moon haven't completely evaded in all their productions.

Foco Novo.   The potential contradiction between the different functions of socialist theatre and a reflection of the Half Moon's dilemma in a touring context is exemplified by Foco Novo. For a number of years in the mid-seventies they alternated more interventionist shows with plays which were more formally derived from the dominant tradition of naturalism. Recently it has dropped the former. Thus, one of its most successful productions, Adrian Mitchell's adaptation of John Berger's *A Seventh Man*, was first and foremost the story of an individual peasant turned immigrant worker, with related commentary. The original book was an uncategorizable montage of photographs, statistics, arguments, poems, reminiscences, essays and evocations about the situation and exploitation of Europe's immigrant workforce. Mitchell commented:

> "If the play had simply used migrant workers to expose capitalism we wouldn't have done it. It tries to understand them — as people. Bad political theatre denies working-class people any form of imagination. Obviously a writer has to be useful but songs, jokes and visions are useful. Everyone in the play has a vision."[10]

A Seventh Man illustrates the particular inflection of Foco Novo: its recognition of an immigrant workforce in this country and its consistent policy of seeking to be a means of expression for this section of society. To date they have premiered plays by Mustapha Matura (one of the most accomplished playwrights writing today but still ignored by the major national companies) and Tunde Ikoli.

7:84.   However, the most consistent project amongst the socialist theatre companies has been that of 7:84 (both English and Scottish companies) headed by the playwright John McGrath. McGrath's career is the reverse of Edgar's, just as the course of 7:84 is the opposite of Edgar's schematic history. McGrath was a successful TV director and writer, wrote film-scripts and had achieved critical recognition in the theatre with *Events While Guarding the Bofors Gun* (1966). Since 1971, however, he has written almost exclusively for the 7:84 companies — a total of some 19 plays and one adaptation. 7:84 began by touring colleges, arts centres and studio theatres with plays which, though they disrupted the mood of naturalism, still belonged within that tradition. However, increasingly the company started using popular entertainment techniques in their productions. At the same time they extended their touring network into clubs, halls and community centres.

The breakaway from the dominant theatre tradition may be seen in retrospect as signalled by John Arden's and Margaretta D'Arcy's *The Ballygombeen Bequest*. Drawing on the vernacular and utilizing agitprop techniques, cartoon characters, songs and ballads, shock-tactics and slapstick comedy, this presented a Marxist perspective on the history of British involvement in Northern Ireland since the war, through the story of the eviction of an Irish sitting tenant from his cottage by an English landlord, Holiday-Cheype, intent on making a quick profit by 'developing' his estate. Verse and prose combined with image to powerful effect, whether in the chilling interrogation scene by British paratroopers (when Padraic, the hero, dies) or in the final scene where Holiday-Cheype and Hogan, another money-grabber, are squabbling over the money across Padraic's coffin. Here the scene resorts to knockabout farce: a pie-fight. Capitalism's criminality is exposed as lunatic farce – but Padraic's ghost is seen to be rising up.

In the next year, 1973, 7:84 broke through into a popular entertainment tradition with the Scottish company's *The Cheviot, the Stag and the Black Black Oil*. This completed the shift away from bourgeois theatre. Since then 7:84 have continued a process of development, sophistication and adjustment, though it has been the Scottish company – and a recent split from it, Wildcat, whose emphasis is more musical – which has been more successful in this project. *The Cheviot* took the form of a ceilidh and was performed to the people of the Highlands and Islands in their village halls. Through sketches both historical and fictional, songs, statistics, monologues and gags, it told the history of the Highlands of Scotland from the Clearances to the present day. This is a history which has often been hidden. It is a history of exploitation, from the introduction of the profitable Cheviot sheep which turned arable land into grazing land and caused unemployment, eviction and emigration, through the later development by an English-based aristocracy of 'their' land for their leisure and in the process degrading grazing land into waste moorland, to the contemporary exploitation of the Highlands by international oil cartels. *The Cheviot* uncovered that hidden history. It gave expression to the feelings of resentment and anger of the local communities. It acted as a spur in the creation of autonomous organizations to defend the interests of the Highland people.

The Cheviot marks the breakthrough into popular entertainment. It also introduces one of the two main themes which, with endless variations, have provided a structural backbone to McGrath's later work: an examina-

"We've cleared the straths." John Bett and Elizabeth MacLennan of 7:84 (Scotland) in *The Cheviot, The Stag and the Black Black Oil* (1973), a musical history of the Scottish Highlands.

tion of the historical development of capitalism and the response of the working class. With the Scottish company this examination has uncovered particular hidden histories within Scotland. With the English company — and this no doubt reflects the lack of any deeply rooted sense of national cultural identity in England — the examination uncovers a global history from the perspective of the international working class.

McGrath's second main theme is central in a play, written around the same time, that remains one of the few dramatic productions of the seventies to fulfil the double Shakespearean injunction — to hold the mirror up to nature and to show the very age and body of the time its form and pressure. Stylistically, though, it remains half-way between naturalism and the more open-ended forms of popular entertainment which were to follow. *Fish in the Sea* was originally written in 1973 for the Liverpool Everyman. It wasn't presented by 7:84 until 1975 when it had some up-datings, some extra songs in the second half and a rock score by Mark Brown.

Set in Liverpool in the early seventies, the complex story focuses on a working class family, the Maconochies, whose life and beliefs are tested by two cataclysmic but contrasting events. One is the occupation of the factory – recently bought up by a multi-national with rationalization plans – where Mr Maconochie works: a determined, organized and concerted action to preserve their jobs by a work-force steeped in a history of struggle. The other is the romantic entanglement of Mary, Maconochie's eldest daughter, with Andy, an anarchistic, violently deranged Glaswegian who, alienated and individualistic, needs to change things by smashing them down, by shooting it out. These opposite poles of working-class action – each in his own way is trying to control an oppressing reality – are set into relief by the sub-plots involving Maconochie's other children and their accommodations to reality: his son's enlisting with the police cadets; Sandra, his second daughter, enthusiastically adopting the role of the consumer-conscious housewife; and Fiona, the youngest, drifting into isolation and a retreat from the reality of relationships.

The two main strands of the plot are connected in a figure from outside the family, Yorry, the local Welsh minister's son, painfully shy but with some of the fire and the fantasy of the poet inside him. Yorry is a student and hopelessly in love with Mary. And it is this figure who embodies McGrath's second theme: the political education and growing to socialist consciousness of the individual. In this instance, Yorry charts the course (exemplary for the generation of '68) from idealistic student revolutionary – "the more powerful I became as a champion of the workers, the further I got away from them. Christ, even behind the locked doors of my childhood at least I had a relationship with the working class: pure terror."[11] – to patient, hard-working committed socialist, a process achieved through grafting in the day-to-day struggle of the factory workers.

This theme had been foreshadowed in the Scottish company's *The Game's a Bogey*. Adapting a variety show format and touring the Labour clubs of the industrialized belt of Scotland, this not only uncovered the hidden history of Red Clydeside and celebrated its most famous leader, John Maclean; it also portrayed representative contemporary characters doing battle with, and trying to rise above, the cynicism and brutality of Glasgow today. Before that, in *Trees in the Wind* and in *Plugged into History*, McGrath offered characters in isolation attempting to face the world's reality. Thus, in *Trees*, Joe – the central character and a violent, articulate, and energetic character in the Andy mould – had confronted the socialist and feminist analyses of the play's three women but had been unable to come to any commitment. Significantly, the play finished with Joe moving through the audience reading passages from Mao. But this resolution was achieved not in terms of character but as dramatic montage.

To say that McGrath's plays centre around one or both of these two themes is not to say that 7:84's shows are limited either in subject matter or in form. The first theme – history told from a socialist perspective – is endless. The second can be used either as the story itself, as in *Yobbo Nowt*, which details the progress of a working-class mother and housewife from enforced domesticity to confident socialist both at work and at home, or as a subsidiary theme and tool of analysis as in *Out of Our Heads*. Here, by means of flashbacks, both the political education of the socialist hero is displayed and the over-riding forces of Scottish culture are analysed. (These latter combine to produce a macho male self-image and a romanticization of and over-reliance on alcohol.)

McGrath's increasing adoption of elements from the working-class entertainment tradition, in particular, its use of songs, anarchic comedy, directness, immediacy and variety, has exposed him to many attacks. Thus David Edgar has said:

> "One of the problems we have is that we don't have a popular tradition that is still feasible, or a revolutionary artistic tradition much beyond Brecht on which to draw. So one of the mistakes that agitprop and a lot of left-wing groups have made is to say we will relate to ordinary people by taking on their forms, as a kind of passport into their consciousness – 'We will write a left-wing Coronation Street'."[12]

That, however, is exactly the project that 7:84 and a number of other groups have undertaken: to revivify a popular working-class and socialist entertainment tradition. This implies a conscious rejection of the despair which, it seems to me, underlies Edgar's analysis, a despair of change. The experience of two other companies should be mentioned here.

Belt & Braces.   Belt & Braces, like 7:84, pioneered the use of rock music in their shows. Indeed, the Belt & Braces Band have developed into semi-autonomous existence and have forged valuable links with Music for Socialism and Rock Against Racism. Having toured on the Continent, in particular Sweden, the company has developed an increasing awareness of the activities of socialist theatre companies on the mainland of Europe. This awareness was partly responsible for their production of Dario Fo's *Accidental Death of an Anarchist*. Fo is an Italian comedian, clown, writer, director and left-wing socialist with an immense working-class following in Italy. Typically he uses popular forms for socialist purposes. *Accidental Death*, which is based on an attempted police cover-up following the death of an anarchist while undergoing interrogation, utilizes farce to present a comedy of counter-information and reduce to absurdity the rationale of the authoritarian right. (Fo, himself, has called the play, "a grotesque farce about a tragic farce".) Despite the Blair Peach case, *Accidental Death* is not, strictly speaking, directly relevant to the British situation. Its importance lies in the fact that it acts as a model for left-wing comedy – fantastical, absurd and satiric – which is directly oppositional to the dominant forms of anti-working-class, racist and sexist

"Now I don't believe in secret police, and I don't believe in torture, but if that bastard doesn't come back I believe we should secretly torture him!" Roland Muldoon of CAST in *Confessions of a Socialist* (1980).

comedy. Its success can be measured by the fact that, some twelve months after its first tour, it transferred to the West End.

CAST. CAST's Roland Muldoon, on the other hand, is the original socialist comedian. Yet, in his wild appearance, his manic energy, in the twisting, stumbling, bubbling rush of his speech patterns, and in the daring leaps of an imagination which is both fantastical and politically rigorously logical, he is in the mainstream of the Music-hall and Northern Variety tradition of anarchic comedians like Frank Randle. Like those comedians he appeals to a sense of localism, though his localism is not that of a geographically defined community but that of the community of the Left, an archipelagic community with which, like all great comedians, he achieves in performance a sense of identity. He is the Left's court-jester, poking fun at their leaders, undercutting their pretensions and loosening the straps on the puritanical straight-jacket which the Left is so prone to impose on its members' behaviour.

This is shown to great effect in *Confessions of a Socialist* – a fantasia about a worker who is thrown on the dole because his job has been automated, blows his redundancy money on a package holiday to Spain and returns to find the revolution has taken place, that automation has taken over and that he is free now to live his dream and go fishing by the canal. The show takes side-swipes at a range of easy targets, including American capitalists and Hughie Green, but it also attacks ultra-democracy and Tony Cliff, one of the leaders of the Socialist Workers' Party. However, its main attack is on one of the sacred cows of the Left: work. In particular, it illuminates the Left's ideological and political confusions surrounding automation, the working class and the work ethic. Importantly though, by situating its criticism from a position within the Left — as indicated by the title — and by developing a sense of identity with the audience, Muldoon expresses, rather than exposes, the Left's doubts and weaknesses. By means of this forced recognition he offers a means of dialectically overcoming them. In this he not only achieves the symbolic victory of all working-class comedy, which for the sacred moment of performance reduces the bosses to grotesque harmlessness, he also streng-thens the audience's resolve to carry that project into reality.

There are, of course, a number of serious difficulties which socialist theatre still has to overcome. Not least of these is the splintering of the Left and the lack of a coherent mass marxist movement. Because of this companies have developed in comparative isolation which has given rise to an illusion of vanguardism. Perhaps because of this, the socialist theatre companies of the seventies have yet to achieve the penetration of the working class that was achieved by the homogeneous, united and Communist Party-dominated Workers' Theatre Movement. On the other hand, that very weakness may yet turn out to be a strength. Perhaps because of the variety of responses the socialist theatre movement contains it shows no sense of being merely a passing theatrical phase or a fallen prey to the sudden shifts in political reality as the Workers' Theatre Movement was.

References

1 Roland Muldoon in an interview in *The Leveller*, April 1978.
2 Chris Rawlence 'Political Theatre and the Working Class' in *Media, Politics and Culture* ed. Carl Gardner (Macmillan, 1979).
3 Richard Seyd 'The Theatre of Red Ladder' *New Edinburgh Review* No. 30, August 1975.
4 Bruce Birchall 'Grant Aid and Political Theatre 1968–77' *Wedge* Nos. 1 & 2, Summer 1977 and Spring 1978.
5 David Edgar 'Political Theatre' *Socialist Review* Nos. 1 & 2, April and May 1978.
6 Roland Muldoon *op. cit.*
7 John McGrath in an interview in *Theatre Quarterly* No. 19/20, 1975.
8 Ernie Dalton in an interview in *Time Out* No. 463, 2–8 March 1979.
9 Chris Rawlence *op. cit.*
10 Adrian Mitchell in an interview in *Time Out* No. 347, 12–18 November 1976.
11 John McGrath *Fish in the Sea* (Pluto Press, 1977).
12 David Edgar in an interview in *Theatre Quarterly* No. 33, 1979.

3 The Personal is Political

Feminism and the theatre

Michelene Wandor

The position of women in the theatre is in many ways similar to their position in other areas of work: clustered around the base of the pyramid in terms of earnings and artistic and administrative power. Very few women reach the top and, in a profession dogged by high unemployment, actresses fare worse than actors. Their average earnings are lower, and most acting companies support twice as many men as women. On the production and administrative side women dominate the traditional servicing fields – secretarial, clerical and publicity. On the artistic side the prime creative positions of writer, director and artistic director are still largely held by men. And whereas women have played a central part in the tradition of writing novels, writing for the theatre has not been something that they have chosen easily. On the technical side of theatre work women are in an even smaller minority; prejudice against women working with technology and a hesitancy on the part of women themselves has ensured that it remains a male-dominated area.

This lack of sexual equality within theatre has consequences for the subject matter of drama. It has meant that most plays written this century embody the male outlook, expressing view and counter-view as a debate conducted very much within a system of aesthetic thinking in which the male is the norm and in which the central protagonist is invariably male. Women, when they do figure, are either adjuncts to those male protagonists or are seen as ciphers for male concerns. Women have rarely been the subjects of drama, either in their own right or in their relations with men. This has also been as true for earlier movements of political theatre. Notions of the working class have been strongly male-defined, and agitational theatre has concentrated on struggles engaged in by men, with the women either being converted to the men's struggle or virtually absent from the political arena altogether.

The situation has not arisen as a result of a massive and conscious conspiracy among men but rather as an often unconscious consequence of the accepted norms of relations between the sexes, based on an ideology which assumes that the biological differences between men and women must necessarily mean that their fields of social activity are different, and that men's work is more significant than women's work.

Despite the expansion of access to education and white-collar and professional jobs after the Second World War, the 'woman's place is in the home' attitude had reappeared sharply – mirroring the same process that happened after the First World War. Wider social change had affected the family more radically than ever in the twentieth century. Increased affluence produced greater isolation for the middle-class housewife, and the break-up of the extended working-class family imposed particular strains on women. Women's magazines during the fifties reflect much of this discontent but it is seen very much as something that individual women can struggle to overcome by being better wives and mothers; it was not until well into the sixties that the real strains on family life came to the surface more clearly.

After the return of the Labour Government in 1964 a number of legislative reforms indicated an implicit recognition that a greater liberalization of the law on family and sexual relations was needed. In 1967 an Abortion Act and an Act partially legalizing male homosexuality were passed (female homosexuality has never been illegal in England). In 1969 the Divorce Reform Act eased conditions for divorce and in 1970 the Equal Pay Act opened up the potential for equal pay for men and women to become a reality by the end of 1975. (In fact women still earn on average about half the amount that men earn.) More efficient methods of contraception, including the pill, made it possible for far more women to contemplate the realistic separation of sex for pleasure from sex for procreation.

The constraints of Victorian Christian morality were steadily giving way to more progressive attitudes and this potential for greater choice for women collided with the cocooned ideology of hearth and home as their natural habitat. The high ideal of the suburban or middle-class housewife was still being held up to women who were actually able to see other horizons. The fact that much of the impetus to modern feminism came from middle-class women (students being groomed for the new affluence) supplies an index of the discrepancy between aspiration and reality which faced all women, but was experienced most acutely by those women who in theory seemed to have furthest to go.

In spring 1970 the first national Women's Liberation Conference was held at Ruskin College in Oxford and four 'demands' were formulated and passed: Equal Pay, Equal Education and Opportunity, 24-hour nurseries, and Free Contraception and Abortion on Demand. The four demands crystallized the particular character of women's oppression, linking her position in the paid workforce with her position in the family, and with individual sexual choice. The Gay Liberation Front didn't come up with such clear political demands but placed the main emphasis on challenging prejudice and discrimination against the right of homosexuals to be open and explicit about their lifestyles. 'Coming out' as gay, publicly and proudly, was paralleled by the way women were beginning to 'come out' with pride rather than shame as women. Both movements emphasized self-activity, protesting against an ideology which trivialized women and gays as inferior and/or 'unnatural'.

From the beginning, theatrical self-expression was part of the feminist and gay movements, who brought with them a new content and new kind of spectacular theatrical imagery. The theatre fell into the pattern of agitprop – the Women's Street Theatre and the Gay Street Theatre Groups both protested against the cattle-market 'beauty' Miss World contests in the Albert Hall in 1970 and the contest was successfully, if briefly, disrupted on television before millions of viewers. A play called *Sugar and Spice* was done by the Women's Street Theatre Group in Trafalgar Square after the first National Women's Liberation March on International Women's Day in 1971. The play was about the oppression and sexual repression of women in the family – a gigantic deodorant and sanitary towel (among other images) defied the usual taboos against acknowledging the intimacies of female body culture, and thus the family and sexuality entered the canon of subject matter of political theatre.

After some more street theatre events the Women's Street Theatre Group addressed itself to more consolidated work. They collectively devised *The Equal Pay Show* in 1972, a cartoon-like analysis with songs which satirized the new legislation, showing how employers could get round it, politicians would manipulate women for their own ends, and male fellow-workers resist it. It was crude, lively and provocative, and brought into directly agitational theatre the subject matter and realities of the lives of working-class women. This has been one important and continuing strand of feminist theatre work, taken up by all-women and mixed groups. Broadside Mobile Workers Theatre, for example, has since 1974–75, had a play based on the Working Women's Charter, which has been used as a programme to improve conditions for women within the labour movement.

A second strand of feminist theatre work developed within Theatre-in-Education, which has represented the younger, radical educational wing within the profession. Many feminist theatre workers have come into fringe theatre work via TIE teams, many of which did some work around feminism. Perhaps the best known (because it is one of the very few political theatre texts published) is *Sweetie Pie*, devised by members of the Bolton Octagon Theatre-in-Education team in 1972. The play took its impetus from the four demands of the WLM; it was structured in the form of a bedtime story, a sort of satirical fairy tale, in which a working-class woman began to see the contradiction between the fairy-tale path her life was supposed to tread and the realities with which she was faced. The

play stated the general case for raised consciousness among women to
their own situation rather than concentrating on a single issue or campaign.

A third strand of feminist theatre has come from within the profession
itself. Among very early work was a semi-surreal play called *Vagina Rex
and the Gas Oven*, by actress and writer Jane Arden, performed at the
Drury Lane Arts Lab in 1969. Jane Arden has since repudiated her interest
in feminism but in 1971 she produced an extraordinary show called
Holocaust, about madness and female archetypes, which drew into it
professional actresses, feminist activists and women working in the other
arts. Between 1970 and 1972 I wrote plays about the Miss World contest,
and about ways in which women are trapped in the family; these were
done on the art fringe and were directly related to my involvement in the
WLM. Another writer, Pam Gems, who had been writing plays through the
fifties and sixties also found a new surge of energy through her contact in
the early seventies with feminist theatre.

The fourth area of feminist influence arose from within the socialist
theatre movement. Red Ladder began work on a 'women's play' in 1972, as
one of the many 'issues' of topical concern; and in terms of both the
expansion of definition of subject matter, and working relations within the
group, it was an important moment in their political theatre work. It is
worth taking a brief look at the play – *A Woman's Work is Never Done* – to
see how it dealt with the way in which an analysis of women has been
systematically evaded by the Left. The group tackled the politics behind
the new feminism, which took on not just the position of women as a
group, but also drew attention to the function of the family in society, and
the roles of men and women within the family. As a theatrical model they
took Brecht's *The Mother*. This is seen by many as an example of a
socialist play which is seriously about a woman. But on closer examination it is clear that for Brecht the figure of the mother is important not as a
female social subject in essence but primarily as a *tabula rasa* of political
consciousness that can be taken to represent a journey from the most
backward political position to the most progressive – 'progressive' as
defined by a struggle located at the point of production and controlled by
men. She 'joins' the 'class' struggle, putting aside her motherly and female
concerns rather than insisting that women too demand struggle.

Red Ladder's play follows the pattern of having a working-class woman
at its centre. Helen moves from an anti-political position to a progressive
position, and in the process takes part in active trade unionism. But she is
different from Brecht's 'Mother'. Firstly, she insists that women at work
have their own needs which the men must recognize; and secondly, she
brings the struggle into her own home. Dave, her husband, has to accept
that if she is to work and be politically active, he must share more equally
in housework and childcare. The play, sometimes crudely, sometimes

A Woman's Work is Never Done, Red Ladder's collectively written play about sexism.

wittily and subtly, brings together the possibilities of socialism and feminism informing each other, without playing down the conflicts and difficulties of the attempt.

As the new feminist and gay consciousness spread slowly, the need developed for cultural work which would reflect the change in attitudes. In 1972 *Spare Rib* (a monthly feminist magazine) and *Gay News* were founded and both were welcomed by their constituency audiences as well as reaching a wider public.

In the spring of 1973 a group of women began to discuss the idea of organizing a multi-media event for women. However, this developed rapidly into a proposal for a season of plays by and about women. A series of meetings drew a mixture of interests – feminists interested in using theatre as a vehicle for propaganda, and professional theatre workers concerned to extend opportunities for women. The meetings came to fruition in the autumn of 1973 in a season of 'women's theatre' put on at the Almost Free theatre in London. The plays were written, directed and stage-managed by women, though men were in some of the productions. It was a season which had as its cohesive centre a frustration with the limited opportunities available for women, and served as a focal point for women to come together to argue about the best way to tackle the problem. The season was very successful and out of it emerged two groups, which represented a more coherent development from the scattered and sporadic feminist theatre work done so far.

Monstrous Regiment in their first play *Scum* (1976) which viewed the Paris Commune through the eyes of the washer-women.

In 1974 the Women's Theatre Group began work, continuing in the spirit of some of the earlier Women's Street Theatre Group, but more focused in its content and its audience. Their main work has been to bridge some of the gaps between Theatre-in-Education work and adult touring agitprop. The first two years of their work involved shows on sex education, work opportunities and a documentary on the equal pay strike of women workers at the Trico windscreen wiper factory in London. They have always been an all-female group, continuing the principle of feminist self-determination without dependence on men, and concentrating their energies on raising the consciousness of young women, extending their self-confidence and encouraging them to explore more positive options in their lives. Like many agitprop groups, they built up their audiences carefully, worked collectively in devising their shows, and always followed them with discussions. The format of the shows was rooted in a simple naturalism, derived in part from the TV naturalism format, interspersed with songs, and with the message clearly punctuating the plays. The function of the naturalism was not simply to provide new material in a familiar format but also implicitly to assert the friendship and conversation and struggle of women as positive and valuable in its own right. In addition, the provocation of being an all-female group has produced its own value. Members of their audiences are surprised that they can carry heavy weights, control their work, organize their shows – a reaction which shows how much people still assume that men run everything. Since 1978 the Women's Theatre Group has begun to explore an area of work which has fitted more into the concept of touring studio theatre – commissioning plays from women writers, and working with outside directors and designers, all of them women. At the moment their work is divided between the educational, youth-oriented work, and the adult, art theatre circuit.

The second group which emerged from the Almost Free season called itself the Women's Company. Run by women, it also included men, but its core consisted of a changing group of professional women theatre workers, who were collectively cautious about claiming political status for their work. Instead, they concentrated on propagandizing for increased work opportunities for women within the profession. The Women's Company only lasted for a brief time; it performed in London fringe theatres, and its underlying principles were similar to those of the better known Monstrous Regiment, which was founded in late 1975 by a group of fringe actresses fed up with their secondary roles in fringe/political theatre. They are a mixed group, with women in the majority. They tour the art-studio theatre circuit and their main intention has been to do plays which focus more heavily on the female rather than the male experience. Their first two plays were commissioned about women in history – the first about women in the Paris Commune in 1871, the second about seventeenth-century witchcraft. After that they changed direction, doing two cabarets, in which they controversially explored the self-presentation of the female glamour image onstage. Their skill as a professional fringe group has indicated how much scope there is for similar work – plays whose subject matter is seen explicitly from the female point of view.

In 1975 the Almost Free hosted a season of gay plays, designed along the lines of the previously successful women's theatre season. The plays were all-male – and the season was the start of Gay Sweatshop. It wasn't until 1976 that lesbians became part of Gay Sweatshop, with a play about lesbian 'coming out' called *Any Woman Can* by Jill Posener. From that time Gay Sweatshop has remained an umbrella group in which the men and women sometimes work on shows together and sometimes work on all-male or all-female plays.

The relationship between the work done by Gay Sweatshop and attitudes to homosexuality within traditional theatre is an interesting one. Camp has long been an accepted element in entertainment – both as a component in humour and as a tactic whereby the presence of homosexuality in the theatre is recognized and contained. There has been a tolerated ghetto of male gay social life within the theatre, following the general social pattern of male activity being more visible and seen as significant. The lesbian ghetto has been smaller and far less visible. Within certain forms of entertainment the camp or the drag queen has been used as a form of ghetto humour which at best is ambivalent in its attitude to women, at worst is downright contemptuous and misogynistic. Within the gay movement men and women share many forms of oppression but they have also to deal with the fact that all men in society are brought up to consider themselves as superior to women within their own class, and the desire of lesbians to express areas of concern of their own has led them at times to create their own theatre. Gay Sweatshop has done other shows on lesbian 'coming out', and a play on women and custody, which linked discrimination against lesbians with the general pressures on mothers in our society to toe the family norm.

The work of both these strands of feminist theatre has been rooted in realism; in the last couple of years feminist theatre has expanded to develop another theatrical strand. The early street theatre used expressionist imagery, and dotted around the early seventies were examples of more anarchic satire/cabaret forms used by feminists: a feminist satire called *Sistershow* in Bristol in 1972, and the sexually aggressive pre-punk *Sadista Sisters* in 1974. But since the beginning of 1978 a series of small, all-women groups have formed, which show both a difference in theatrical direction and an implicitly different approach to the impact of feminism within theatrical work.

The social-realist based work seeks to present an alternative picture of women's lives onstage to the trivialized and stereotyped one prevalent in the established theatre. The new work tackles another aspect of the representation of women in our dominant culture: that of female sexuality as it is presented to us through advertising and sexual objectification. As groups they don't necessarily begin with that as a consciously worked-out policy but they are interesting because their impact is to question that imagery of the sexually feminine, sometimes to undermine it, and to replace it with a form of female humour that revels in its self-confidence. The potency of their effect lies in the way they subvert the high bourgeois image of sexuality – enshrined in the concept of glamour.

Female sexual glamour falls into two categories: the pre-marriage sexuality which is pure, demure, or sophisticated and challenging, but which above all sets women up in competition with each other for the attentions of men; secondly, there is the post-marriage sexuality in which women are more important for a nurturing cosiness – still in terms of their service to men and children. The up-market versions of these presents us with women who are glossy, a part of the leisure world of luxury consumption. As such women represent both a possession and a symbol of that world for men.

The new groups implicitly challenge the rigidity of this impossible imagery by sending it up, defusing it, denying it and creating an alternative form of female self-presentation based on confidence rather than self-denigration. The punning, ironic names of the groups give a clue to their content: Clapperclaw, Hormone Imbalance, Bloomers, Cunning Stunts, Beryl and the Perils. One of the most successful of these shows was *Dennis the Menace* by the Perils. The show was about women and sex – hetero and homo, individual and coupled. The four performers used the pre-pubescent comic-book imagery of the *Dandy/Beano* genre. They took the idea of dressing up – bizarre clothes and streaked faces – to send up the whole theatrical and everyday vocabulary of women's physical appearance to give them a freedom to cavort, use clown antics, acrobatics, playing around with the notion of the fixed, glossy feminine by undermining it at every move. As a theatrical style it has great potential in the task of creating a female-influenced humour which discovers its own objects of wit, instead of women being always the butt of popular comedy.

Cunning Stunts!

The work of these varied groups is the backbone of the presence of feminism in the theatre, as they have control over the form, content, organization and distribution of their work. The position of freelance individual theatre workers for whom feminism is important, is more difficult. In the second half of the seventies far more women were writing for the theatre, having been encouraged and given opportunities by fringe feminist companies. Not all the writers would call themselves feminist but there is no doubt that their contact with feminist or women-dominated groups has given them greater confidence both as writers and in terms of their interest in exploring women's experience on stage. Apart from my own writing, plays by Pam Gems, Caryl Churchill, Cherry Potter, Bryony Lavery, Melissa Murray and Donna Franceschild have benefited from contact with feminist companies. Other writers, such as Gilly Fraser, Olwen Wymark, Val McDermid, Victoria Wood and Louise Page have written particularly vividly about women and will hopefully continue to do so.

The heightened awareness among women theatre workers has also been reflected in industrial organization. In the second half of the seventies a feminist theatre study group met over a period of about three years in London and, in part due to its impetus, a Women's Sub-committee was formed within Equity. Recently, at different times, actresses at the National Theatre and in the Royal Shakespeare Company have expressed frustration with their position as a minority in the company with relatively less rewarding roles than the men. But these are only small beginnings; changing fundamental attitudes within theatre both to equal participation by women and to a changed emphasis in subject matter, involves men facing the fact of their own dominance. It is not an easy issue to struggle with and it means that for a long time to come (economic climate and subsidy willing) there will be a need for all-women and feminist groups. The answer does not lie in simply commissioning successful playwrights (at the moment almost all male) to write plays with more parts for actresses, but in allowing and actively encouraging positive discrimination towards women in all areas of theatre work.

The political theatre movement functions in a number of inter-related complex ways. At one level it is a movement of cultural protest, which seeks to challenge the values of the dominant culture and to create alternatives. But it also functions as an informal proving ground for the industry as a whole. The commercial and larger subsidized companies have always taken workers, plays and subject matter from the experimental fringe where it has seemed to them commercially valid to do so. The amount of cross-fertilization is small but nevertheless the channels are there.

Feminism within theatre offers its own very specific impetus but it has further implications for theatre in general. One of the early slogans of the Women's Liberation Movement was that 'the personal is political'. Like all slogans it is open to misunderstanding and abuse but at its core is the conviction, derived from the specifics of women's oppression, that there is no detail, however small and intimate, of social and individual life, which does not have a wider political meaning, and is therefore subject to change. The resurgence of feminism has introduced new questions about the relationship between the individual and his/her society and the nature of political change, and it is from this source that we might see a new definition of political subject matter for theatre.

4 The Public-going Theatre
Community and 'ethnic' theatre

Naseem Khan

Community Theatre

The late sixties saw not only the development of the fringe but also the beginnings of community theatre. As Su Braden asserts strongly: "Concern for the separation of art and artists from the rest of society, expressed by a growing concentration on new ways of putting art and artists back into social contexts, may be seen as the stamp of this decade. [The seventies]"[1] However, the movement of the present has been built upon the concern of the past, and the first early stirrings of new ideas about the relationship between art and audience, product and process, occurred long before the late sixties.

Ten years before the theatrical watershed of 1968, discontent with, above all, current conventions of writing for the theatre was rife. But this discontent stretched beyond just writing, with the work of Joan Littlewood in the unglamorous community of Stratford East. In *Encore*, in November 1957, Lindsay Anderson had written: "The development of a new kind of theatre is intimately bound up with the development of a new kind of audience. [This] carries us to the need for a new conception of the relationship between art and audience, a total change in the cultural atmosphere."[2] *Encore* called this new theatre 'Vital Theatre'.

In the early sixties, Charles Marowitz continued the argument: "What has to be found in the theatre is a new urgency, a new imperative, a new and better reason why thousands of people now glued to the Box or snug in cinema seats should forsake these diversions and attend the live theatre."[3] More practically, with Centre 42, Arnold Wesker attempted to attract a working-class audience.

The explosion of the fringe in the late sixties continued this development. But though venues like Jim Haynes' Arts Lab or the Ambiance in Queensway attracted a different audience from that of traditional theatre, they were more conscious of the need for good new writing than in the idea of community theatre. Indeed, this was still the bias with slightly later ventures like the Half Moon in Tower Hamlets and Wakefield Tricycle in a King's Cross pub (both started in 1972).

In fact, the early fringe can be seen to have had its precursors, largely unsung, in the Sunday night theatres and small theatre clubs set up between the wars. Their aim was to counter the dominance of an extremely complacent West End, to present new work and provide young actors with challenge and stimulus. The way Norman Marshall, the historian of the club theatres, describes them – in particular his own tiny theatre, The Gate – is reminiscent of the later fringe:

> "The stage was so close to the audience that those sitting in the front row could – and sometimes did – sit with their feet resting on the edge of the stage. At first, it was terrifying for an actor to have to play a long emotional scene with the spectators sitting at little more than arm's length, but actually the advantages of this outweighed the disadvantages . . . The actor could play far more rapidly and intimately at The Gate than is possible in a normal sized theatre . . . On the other hand, because of this extreme intimacy between stage and auditorium, insincerity was at once detected by the audience. The Gate mercilessly revealed any sort of trickery or stageyness." [4]

Today that description may still be apt for studio theatres like the Bush. It hardly applies to community theatre.

Of the early groups, only Inter-Action started out as a community theatre company with its non-theatre-based Dogg's Troupe, a flexible group of performers who worked in streets, hospitals, old people's homes. (Inter-Action was the North London based parent company of the Ambiance Lunch Hour Theatre Club and the experimental TOC as well as of Dogg's Troupe.)

In 1969, Interplay, originally a Leeds-based off-shoot of Inter-Action, was formed; but the major development of community theatre did not properly begin until 1970–72. In that short time a large number of companies were established. West London Theatre Workshop began, presenting variety/documentaries on political themes, like their show on pensions which was performed to senior citizens around a circuit of working men's clubs, polytechnic halls and other non-theatre venues. In Wandsworth, Christine Eccles formed Mayday Theatre, which presented a number of local issue plays, including several by Jeremy Seabrook and Michael O'Neill. In 1972 the Half Moon opened in its old synagogue building in the East End, aiming to present political community theatre, while in Leeds the General Will was formed. This was originally a socialist political theatre group but after some years it developed into a resource-based organization available for use by action groups within the Bradford locality who wished to make theatre.

Definitions of community theatre, as we shall see, are vague and overlapping. Matters aren't helped by the way that individual companies have changed over the years. Wakefield Tricycle, for instance, which for years had no base and an extremely diverse policy that included both Sam Shepard at the King's Head and housing documentaries in trades union clubs, has recently been assigned the large Foresters Hall in the London Borough of Brent, which they intend to develop as a community theatre centre. Another example is Chat's Palace in Hackney. Set up by Freeform, it involved the local community to such an extent that the group is on the point of passing over responsibility for the theatre aspect of the centre to local people. Another example is the early history of The (Brighton) Combination from fringe theatre to campaigning touring group to a community theatre company based in South London. (See Chapter 1.) The Combination's move to the Albany in Deptford was a response to their audiences. The building suited their needs: not an arts centre but a community focus in an area deprived and wrenched apart by the Blitz and subsequent rebuilding. Here The Combination aims to offer more than theatre – they run courses in pottery, music, dance, silk-screen printing, etc – and more than theatre in the building, but also out in the locality.

This desire to perform to different, non-theatre-going audiences, and to engage them in a different relationship, is not unique to community theatre but shared widely across the fringe. One of the tenets of the fringe was that theatre should escape from its own buildings, and by the early seventies a nationwide circuit of halls, colleges, arts labs and centres, and local non-traditional venues had been built up. But through the seventies this aspect – that theatre should escape out into the 'community' – has been taken up very widely throughout the industry. Thus the Arts Council touring section has helped to develop a small-scale touring network – though one composed of arts centres, colleges and the studios of rep theatres in the main. Various Regional Arts Associations have developed their own networks of non-traditional venues. The Royal Shakespeare Company has a unit that tours to similar venues and the National Theatre has an Outreach programme. At the same time, regional touring companies have been set up, like EMMA by the East Midlands Arts Association, to take good mainstream work to village halls and other local venues.

All this compounds the question: what exactly constitutes Community Theatre? And while it is true that ten years ago nobody would have known what was meant by 'community theatre' (or, indeed, 'ethnic theatre') at all, nowadays there are many different definitions and interpretations of the term. 'Community', as Raymond Williams has noted, was one of the vogue words of the seventies. But whereas originally 'community', though always referring to a series of overlapping concepts, implied an identification with the under-privileged and the local, it has now been so thoroughly annexed by everyone that it can mean almost anything, from 'the gay community' to the Commonwealth's 'community of nations', from small interest groups to society at large.

'Community theatre' is in even worse peril, for it has only developed as a form of theatre during the time that the specific meanings of 'community' were being eroded. This erosion threatens the whole idea of community theatre as something different: it becomes just the same as the National Theatre only smaller, less spectacular and generally, inferior. (The position with 'ethnic theatre' is even worse, for everyone is 'ethnic'.)

However, the beginnings of a definition of community theatre can be found in its original motive. This was both selfish and altruistic. It was both the desire to find a more fulfilling context for one's craft and the desire to carry theatre to the theatrically deprived. Most importantly, however, the Wesker lesson had been learned by proxy. Taking the high spots of the cultural tradition was considered irrelevant and, even worse, patronizing. Cultural missionaries were out. (The danger is that the products deemed relevant might be, in actual fact, even more patronizing.) Community theatre is not about making Shakespeare more widely available: this at least distinguishes it from the touring operations of the RSC and from schools matinees at the local rep.

A number of qualifying factors have from time to time been isolated. Firstly, there is the idea that a group should have a base in, identify itself with and be identified with, a certain distinct area. However, this does not quite square with the facts. Were that the case, then any regional rep could call itself community theatre. And where would that definition put TOOT 2 (The Other Oxfordshire Theatre 2) or Medium Fair, both of whom have no base and tour widely in Oxfordshire and Devon respectively? It would also put out of court Avon Touring, Word and Action, M6, Live Theatre. Clearly, 'to have a base' in a defined area cannot be identified with having a building that is specifically used for presenting theatre. Rather it is indicating a different set of relations between theatre (or theatre company) and public. It is 'putting people before buildings'. That is a handy slogan – but an inadequate definition.

A second theory is that content is what matters. Jenny Harris, artistic director of the Albany, has said: "All community theatre is issue-based."[5] But this seems to raise more difficulties than it disposes of. EMMA, for instance, tours with material that is tailored to its geographical area, presenting shows about local sons like D. H. Lawrence and Captain Cook. Orchard Theatre in the West Country includes in its touring repertoire plays in praise of cider and documentaries about itinerant Methodist preachers of the area in the early twentieth century as well as the more classically based plays *Miss Julie* and *Vicar of Wakefield*. But does this make those companies community theatres? At the same time, groups like Inter-Action's Dogg's Troupe – which are indubitably community theatre companies – base their work not on issues but on games. And The Combination's recent *Mutiny on the M1* (about a pop group) is hardly a campaigning issue.

More commonly, though, community theatre – and the content of its productions – is thought to be 'relevant' to its community. The dictionary definition here is "bearing upon, connected with, pertinent to". Clearly, again, this theory is pointing towards a different relation between theatre and community. It points towards a relationship which is closer, more direct, more important perhaps; a relationship where theatre is an integral part of the community. But as a definition, 'relevant' is notably slippery; besides, who is to say exactly what is relevant to whom? And could not the theatrical genre developed by, and popular with, the regional reps – the local documentary – be relevant? Again, clearly, though such concerns may point towards a definition, they do not clarify one.

What, in fact, distinguishes Medium Fair from Orchard Theatre (or even

Members of The Combination performing at an anti-racist festival in Deptford, April 1978. The Combination and its base, The Albany, were also involved in hosting Rock Against Racism and were active in other forms of anti-racist struggle.

Footsbarn and Avon Touring) is the issue of participation. It is this that makes a touring community theatre group distinct from a touring regional theatre company, a stable community theatre/arts group from a similarly stably based repertory theatre. 'Participation' in itself is another confusing word. In the early days of the fringe, the threat of 'participatory drama' spread some alarm and consternation among audiences. Audiences could be (and were) locked up in cages, insulted, embarrassed and manhandled in order to make a dramatic point. Community theatre's 'participation' is of a different order and embodies more basic respect for and less hostility toward those it approaches.

The ways in which groups define their basic intentions differ. Inter-Action, for instance, describes its work as: "The use of different artists within a community to stimulate the participation of people in that particular art-form: usually – and mainly, in the minds of the practitioners – for some form of social improvement."[6] The Combination, who have over the years refined their 'target area', see themselves as: ". . . trying to build young popular theatre for an audience without higher education and the whole bourgeois cultural heritage . . . Participation is really in the meeting of minds in the right environment."[7] Medium Fair believes that: "Artistic activity can lend a dimension to community action which will involve more people in ways which are, potentially at least, extremely powerful. And furthermore, that the combination of art and action, the aesthetic and the pragmatic, is a way of enabling a community to strengthen its sense of identity, while simultaneously providing actual, concrete improvements."[8] TOOT has a similar belief. Its strength, asserts Julian Hilton, one of TOOT's members: ". . . lay in the diversity of its activity and depth of its roots in well-defined communities: it acted as an agent for many and complex needs for (and feelings of) community."[9] Lastly, the Telford Community Art Project in the West Midlands sees its role as being: ". . . to create opportunities and conditions in which the voice of a community may be expressed creatively, and to help that expression be clear, imaginative and effective by offering a range of artistic skills and experience to local people."[10]

Clearly groups differ in detail (and should do, if they are to reflect their own qualities and the character of the areas). But the consensus is that community theatre is based within a certain defined area, that it provides inhabitants with entertainment, an arts resource service and the possibility of being involved in the process of shaping and mounting a play. Those groups like The Combination who do not base their theatre work on local participation balance that by the nature of their other community arts work. Theatre in general is seen not as an end in itself but as part of a wider programme of arts and community work.

Actual examples will help to clarify things. Consider, for instance, Medium Fair. Begun in 1972 by a lecturer and some students from Exeter

University, Medium Fair tackled a broad front of community theatre activities, including games-based participation pieces with young children; shows relevant to older children, such as a number of short plays linked by songs about juvenile delinquency and the problems of growing up told from the youths' points of view — which toured to youth clubs; music-hall programmes for older people — which toured Old People's Homes; short pub entertainments which mixed songs, very broad comedy and characterization and political satire; and more recognizable plays — though these, like *Pilgrim's Progress*, were influenced by the experimentation of the fringe — for more general audiences. The company was also involved in giving theatre workshops for children and for patients at one of the local mental hospitals.

Originally the group toured shows to some 30–35 Devon venues but the formula became increasingly unsatisfactory to the group. Consequently they devised a scheme of 'Village Visit Weeks'. These consisted initially of extended stays in selected villages during which they both presented their own shows and worked with villagers towards presenting something of their own devising at the end of the week. The ideal achievement of the final product was to give an expression to a self-defined community identity. In Ilsington, for instance, the story of a local ghost became the focus. In Colyton, it was the church bells. (The 'village pieces' were finally set in the format of a concert entertainment, together with games, turns and sing-songs.) Medium Fair aims to act as a catalyst to provide the missing link between past and present so that the present is illuminated by the past. It is not, in itself, an unusual aim nor so different, for instance, from some of Peter Cheeseman's work at Stoke. Where Medium Fair differs is that the themes themselves are chosen, fleshed out and performed by the villagers.

The Malinslee Theatre Group, working under the aegis of the Telford Community Arts Project, work in a broadly similar way. In 1979 project members working with local people created and staged two plays. One, *The Ironbridge Forge, or Who Built the Bridge?* was timed to coincide with the Ironbridge bicentenary. The second sprang from the fact that at that time there was no local doctor, and developed to become a critical look at the National Health Service. Both shows travelled to a range of local venues, from pubs to techs.

It is clear from the stated intentions of the groups that the success or failure of community theatre is assessed by them in non-traditional terms. "There was the chance," said Baz Kershaw of Medium Fair, "that the more skilful the actor, the more discouraged from actually doing anything your audience might be."[11] Theatre is a means to a social effect, the more concrete the better. An instance from the work of Dogg's Troupe can be cited as an example of how things should be. It happened when the group was performing on the streets in the East End. Afterwards, as usual, they made a point of talking to onlookers and suggesting, if they'd enjoyed the event, they initiated local activities themselves. In this case the young mothers claimed that any kind of improvement was impossible and pointed out a group of local tearaways as the reason. They vandalized everything, the women claimed, including the old laundry building they were standing outside. That building had, however, a usable first floor which Inter-Action workers, in conjunction with local social workers, helped acquire for the women to use as a centre. The ever-present kids hovered around downstairs while courses with the women were worked out upstairs, and eventually they were drawn into the video project. The mothers decided to do an initial project on the lack of local provision for young people. A lobby group was set up to renovate downstairs for their use and the mothers also set in motion a number of summer festival and play-scheme plans. The whole process took three years.

To judge the original street show on its artistic merit is to miss the point. Similarly, Medium Fair shows are valuable in what they precipitate. Occasionally this has been considerable, like the acquisition of the Peacock-Cookson Centre by Starcross Village. And Telford see their theatre element in the broader context of murals, processions, community newspaper, festivals and much else. At the same time standards are not irrelevant. Though there is a distinction between community theatre *for* people, e.g. The Combination, TOOT, and community theatre *with* people, e.g. Medium Fair, Telford, neither would last long if they did not attract audiences. In community theatre, as in everything, there must be excellence, but excellence of its own type.

For groups themselves this involves a learning process; mistakes have been made. After all, there are few, if any, precedents in this area. The Combination admits that realistically. On first coming to Deptford, they believed people across all age-ranges would respond to ". . . warm, welcoming, relevant art".[12] Some did, but they were overwhelmingly the young – children, teenagers, the under-35s. Initially The Combination found this demoralizing, but then came to realize that it was important to play to their contemporaries. "We became much more hard-headed and more confident in our art: not so much pandering to what we thought were our audience's tastes. Consequently the work became less pressured, less guilt-ridden – more interesting . . . For five years, everyone was blinkered by the flat cap image."[13] The Combination also discovered through experience that, on the whole, exposés of social ills did not go down well, however sharp and witty; and that the work had to be theatrically good – nothing amateur and tatty. For the comparisons people tended to make were with the sophisticated products of television.

Issues, according to Ed Berman, were never to the forefront of Inter-Action's theatrical work with the Dogg's Troupe: "Issue is what motivates people to do it. Where and how and to whom has always been more

Inter-Action's Dogg's Troupe on the streets issuing their 'Bonkers Property Shares' in support of the campaign to save Covent Garden.

important to us than what.'' For Berman, shows work best when they are non-specific and elicit a personal response or interpretation. An event about moonmen, for instance, has been taken as a metaphor for anything from meeting new people to strangers in the area. Unlike many other community groups, he believes developments have been much as he predicted. They have improved in the quantity rather than in the quality of their work and the orientation has changed: "We always had a very clear idea of how things should be. However, in the early days there were lots of one-off visits to other sites. There was only about a 20% follow-up. Now the proportion has shifted radically. We have learnt that theatre is just a first step, and not art for art's sake." [14]

It is commonly thought that there is a polarization within culture today between, on the one hand, the 'mass art' of the culture industry – the products of television, film and music industries in which art is indistinguishable from technology – and, on the other hand, the individual, humanist art of the more traditional art-forms. The former can be seen as brazenly commercial, immediate and apparently ephemeral, as 'appealing to the lowest common denominator' and as authoritarianly imposed on, and outside the control of, those media's audiences. In contrast the latter can be seen as elitist, bourgeois and as essentially peripheral to the decision-making processes of society. While in saying that art has eternal value and that creativity is the property of the artist, traditional art also puts itself outside the control of its audiences.

This dichotomy presents an unenviable dilemma for both 'artists' and 'people'. Community theatre (and community arts) is attempting to create a third alternative which avoids the limitations of both the culture industry and traditional art. Its central difference is that the communication of meaning and value is seen as a two-way flow between 'artists' and 'people' – and not the one-directional process of either of the above. To achieve this the defining characteristic of community theatre is 'participation'. This can, as we have seen, take two broadly different directions – one in which the artist participates much more fully in his/her local community; the other in which the community participates much more fully in the creation of art.

The major problem at present is that all these explorations are journeys into new ground and need time. They need subsidy; but because their activities cut across all existing definitions they have been subsidized from a variety of state departments. In the harsh economic climate and the prevailing political philosophy of today these are under threat. So several community projects which were developed through the Manpower Services Commission, or used STEP money, are being cut back. Others, which depend on local authority backing, are also under threat. Cut-backs in education will undoubtedly affect the work that many community theatre groups do with schools and young people. And the whole policy of the devolution of community arts by the Arts Council to the Regional Arts Associations raises troubling questions. (It is worth noting that five community theatre groups in the North have recently had their funding withdrawn.)

The survival and growth of community theatre no longer depends on the (increasing) skills of its practitioners but on the ability and willingness of funding bodies both to recognize the different skills required and to continue supporting developments in this area. Were this not to take place the result could be the destruction of an area of art that, at its very best, is a potent and regenerative social force.

'Ethnic' Theatre

If 'community theatre' is a baffling term then what is one to make of 'ethnic theatre'? The phrase is, of course, an elision, a handy shortening of the unwieldy 'ethnic minority communities' theatre'. And there is a lot to say for throwing the term out wholesale. Like 'community theatre', it has had its use as a spotlight. It has thrown light on an area of work that had previously gone uncategorized and hence unnoticed. But while at the heart of community theatre – however diverse its outward appearance – there is a broadly consistent aim, the same cannot be said of ethnic theatre. What is there in common between an Armenian social comedy and dramatized memories of Caribbean children of their coming to Britain?

At the same time, how is the work of the Tara Arts Group, for instance, different from that of Common Stock? Both work in English; both use the experiences of the people to whom they play, and seek to clarify and illuminate them through drama; both work in community venues. Is the fact that the Tara Arts Group is Asian and deals with Asian issues a reason for boxing it into 'ethnic theatre' along with Poles, Cypriots and all the other peoples classified as 'minorities' in Britain? A long time ago I remember doing a piece for *Time Out* to be entitled 'Black Theatre'. "Do you call the other stuff White Theatre?" I was asked caustically.

Unlike 'community theatre', 'ethnic theatre' is not only a vague and meaningless portmanteau term. It is also dangerous, distancing and potentially ghettoizing. It diminishes the work to the level of exotica, and pushes it out onto the peripheries of British life. It has no place on the periphery: it is no new phenomenon. Let us first examine the roots. As with community theatre, they are embedded in social and political fact: in this case, the fact of immigration. Early rumblings of immigration restrictions in the fifties led to a dramatic increase in people coming to Britain from Commonwealth countries. This was augmented by events like the expulsion of Indian communities from Kenya and Uganda in the sixties and early seventies.

We are now in the fortunate situation of having a variety of different communities settled in Britain. I cannot think of a single one that does not have some form of artistic activity: Chinese music, West Indian folk dance, Indian classical music, Armenian theatre, Pakistani public poetry bonanzas and so on. While a lot of the theatre activity is sporadic, ad hoc, and dependent on the energies of a relatively few committed people, there are areas that are better-established and more consistent. The theatre has developed side by side with immigrant communities. For example, in Birmingham in the forties, when the Asian population was in three figures, cultural activity was the prerogative of the Indian student population who performed to its own members and the small settler community. West Indian drama had a foothold in, most notably, London's West Indian Students' Centre, which provided the focus for a great deal of creative talent that later went back to develop as significant Caribbean writers, playwrights, poets and performers (as well as future politicians). However, it is fair to say that neither of these activities had much of a wider constituency. They were back-home, back-room activities: valuable, but private.

Black theatre.   As communities increased, became more secure and had second-generation offspring growing up in Britain, things changed. There had been the occasional black theatre/dance group in the fifties but the first to take root – however tenuous – was the Dark and Light Theatre in Brixton. The brainchild of a talented Jamaican actor, Frank Cousins, it was primarily a response to the dire situation in 1970, when it was founded, of black professional actors. It was a period in which casting, in television and the theatre, was rigorously monoracial. Even Equity's Coloured Actors' Committee, however limited its scope, had died away. (It was not until 1975 that Equity's newly constituted Afro-Asians Committee emerged.)

So firstly, the Dark and Light set out to provide a range of experience for black actors and actresses in, as the name implies, a multiracial setting. Secondly, it aimed to provide theatre for a community hitherto without it. In its three and a half years of life, the Dark and Light went some way to meeting its first aim. However, it also encountered all the problems that black theatre and, to a similar extent, other theatre groups springing out of new communities, were to face. Funding was extremely limited and the pool of actors was predictably unreliable: if a television spot turned up, he/she would more often than not drop the badly paid theatre job that would anyway have played to only a handful. (This is one of the reasons why black theatre began to gain a name for unreliability.) Audiences were not good, which was again hardly surprising. The Dark and Light was bringing a traditionally Western theatrical product to a community that had little tradition of theatre. Touring was some solution, since local organizations like community relations councils 'bought' shows and were responsible for selling them. But the wages were so low, actors reluctant to leave London and the strains of touring great.

The Dark and Light's thin shows in their home base were in striking contrast to occasional grassroots community shows that used their building. I remember a rough and ready electric evening provided by a local youth group, the Fasimbas. Their sketches, a hilarious and pungent analysis of the black situation in Britain, played to a packed house of parents and peers. Again, a touring one-off production of *Smile Orange*, a comedy with teeth by Trevor Rhone, collected good audiences.

Nevertheless the Dark and Light experience was to prove important; for it not only provided – as it had set out to do – a range of roles, but it also proved that it could be done and that some public funding at least was there to support it. Eventually Frank Cousins and his able colleague

The youth-orientated and influential Black Theatre of Brixton in the mid-seventies.

Manley Young bowed out, and the venture turned into the more youth-oriented Black Theatre of Brixton under the initial directorship of Jamal Ali, Norman Beaton and Rufus Collins. Ali's own group RAPP metamorphosed into a new compact group, which toured with an imaginative mix of poetry, satire and music.

The ripples spread wider and other groups followed – Wall Theatre, Grasshopper, Brixton Arts Theatre, L'Ouverture, Legba, Omnibus, Temba, Centrestage, Birmingham's Black Expression, Bristol's West Indian Drama Group, community initiatives in Leeds and Nottingham. Frequently there have been quick changes of direction within groups and not infrequently groups have vanished (Calabash, Theatre of Black Youth, Hewanorra, Acacia). Above all there has been the establishment in Islington of the Keskidee centre, a rambling dilapidated mission school, which quickly became a base for productions. In 1976 it reopened after a comprehensive face-lift and the theatre, under Rufus Collins, came into its own. Keskidee has presented regular seasons of its own plays – a range of African, Caribbean and black American work – and developed its own style. For much of the time they have had a core of increasingly seasoned actors.

The proliferation of groups, as well as the existence of the stable Keskidee, has created a fertile atmosphere for black theatre. There are now far more experienced black actors (and no excuse for casting directors to claim, as they did in the past, that no one good existed so they were forced to black-up a white actor). At the same time, the fact of those actors and the feeling of expanding possibilities in the theatre has created the conditions for the emergence of writers: Mustapha Matura, Michael Abensetts, Jimi Rand, T Bone Wilson, Alfred Fagon, Tunde Ikoli. Television has opened its doors slowly to writers dealing with West Indian life in Britain; white writers have slowly begun writing parts for black actors. The range of work is great — from group-concocted mirrors of local life like Black Expression's to Temba's more mainstream presentations of Fugard, Biko and David Halliwell; from dialect West Indian plays to African expressionism. The audiences are critical and demanding. Predominantly they are young.

The change from the early seventies is not simply one of scale. It is not just a matter of more groups, more theatres, more audiences. The focus of the work has changed. Ten years ago plays were designed to show the paces of actors (from *Emperor Jones* to *The Blood Knot*). Today they overwhelmingly reflect local life, use dialect and do not imitate the West End. The Fasimbas in the early seventies were a first example of the type of work being put together by Early Start, Black Expression, the United Caribbean Association of Leeds. Their shows are portmanteau untidy plays, drawn from experience, both fighting and funny work. In purely dramatic terms they lack a lot, but in terms of immediacy, relevance and response they are strong.

One major reason why black theatre in Britain shows signs of healthy expansionism is the fact of language. The English language, however modified it may be in dialect, has provided broader horizons than exist for other forms of ethnic community theatre. It has enabled work to be seen more widely; it has been easier for art-funding bodies to comprehend than, say, Marathi theatre.

Polish theatre.   Although in theory the urge to maintain a language and the culture that goes with it should be a potent force for the creation of vital theatre, this does not seem to have been the case in most other communities. There are, of course, long-established groups, particularly in the Polish community, which established itself in Britain during the last war. The theatrical standards of groups like Polish Artists Equity and the youth theatre, Syrena, are high and their staging imaginative. Community support for them is strong. However, they face a diminishing future. Both groups find it increasingly difficult to enlist young people with adequate spoken Polish (despite the efforts of the many Polish Saturday schools). At the same time it is inevitable that the bulk of their material has to come from Poland and hence be immediately divorced from life and change in Britain. Obviously some plays do have universal relevance. But nevertheless, a theatre without young writers is a limited theatre. This is a disadvantage that, in differing ways, both Cypriot and Asian theatre have faced.

Cypriot theatre. Cypriot theatre in Britain is the product of one man, George Evgeniou. In 1957 he started his Theatro Technis in a Camden Town garage. Plays were solely in Greek and dealt with concerns touching the Greek-Cypriot community: Junta politics, racism, sweatshop employment. He has had a long and – apart from his core of colleagues – a lonely struggle. As with West Indians, Cypriots have little tradition of theatre, especially the rural immigrants to whom Evgeniou was wanting to play. And, like West Indians, the first generation of immigrants set themselves a life of intensive toil. There was little time, energy or inclination to go to the theatre. Evgeniou nevertheless persisted and slowly expanded his base of support. What has changed his theatre's situation are two events that on the face of it boded nothing, in differing degrees, but tragedy. The Turkish invasion of Cyprus in 1974 meant not only some increase in the local Cypriot population, it also meant that far more young Cypriots already in Britain felt drawn to close ranks within their community. Evgeniou's wider social work programme catered for refugees (particularly the elderly) and drew on wider young voluntary help. Inevitably they were also drawn to his theatre. His group acquired new blood. It increasingly played in English rather than Greek (the Greek of the young is anyhow of not too high a standard). In 1977 Evgeniou took his young group back to Cyprus, where they played in refugee camps. It has also begun to consider plays on relevant themes written by non-Cypriot writers (such as *Dowry With Two White Doves* by Nick McCarty and an adaptation of the Don Camillo stories). The second 'disaster' was the loss of the Technis premises in York Way, north of King's Cross. It was a loss that Evgeniou and his group fought fiercely, from street to council chamber. They were unsuccessful but in the event this has proved to be a good thing. The new building which they now inhabit is more accessible, less bleak and more compact.

With his Theatro Technis George Evgeniou has created a base for the issues and concerns of the Greek-Cypriot community in London.

Asian theatre.   Asian theatre has had a similar battle to find its audiences. It has been a slow growth – far slower than the more familiar and acceptable Asian art forms of music and dance. Partly this has again been lack of tradition. Very largely, however, it has been due to the unflattering light in which the acting profession (particular the film stars) are regarded back home. Actresses in the early days were like gold-dust. Groups such as Harbhajan Virdi's in Southall in the sixties had virtually to do without them. It was hardly surprising. An insecure community was not going to take chances with its daughters' futures for the sake of a play.

It was also a political tragedy, ironically enough, that gave new blood to the Asian theatre in Britain. When the Asian communities were displaced from Kenya and Uganda, they brought with them to Britain very different social mores. More westernized and less socially constrained, theatre had been a not uncommon pastime for both men and women. For the first time there was a significant number of people with some dramatic experience, as well as an audience appreciative of Gujarati theatre. Groups were quick to emerge – Leicester's Literary Arts and Lights, Birmingham's L & P Enterprises, London's Indian National Theatre, the drama section of the Bharatiya Vidya Bhavan.

As with the Polish theatre, Asian theatre faces the problem of language. Plays are performed in Gujarati and have been Indian imports. Those that I have seen have been essentially drawing-room comedies, and have tended to reinforce the consciousness of a certain sort of Indian society and the values that inform it. They have dealt with meaty themes – generational conflict, arranged marriages – and have included passages of strong emotion as well as the obligatory slapstick interludes, but by the end accommodation has always been reached within the existing value structure.

Stressing the significance of the Gujarati theatre does not mean that there have not been other initiatives in other forms of language theatre. The Maharashtrian Theatre Group has been performing its annual play for many years. Shamsuddin Agha has long been the driving force of his Asian Artists Association who perform in Hindi/Urdu. (One of their productions is a translation of Agatha Christie's *Dial M for Murder*.) Ros Lyle in Birmingham trained many Asian youngsters in her Hindi-speaking East-West Community Theatre Group. The Bengali theatre is slowly developing. Bangladeshis brought up in Britain (many of them at one time involved with the drama course of Amar Bose and the Bengali Artists Association) are beginning to use drama in the East End of London as part of a wider programme of young community action.

But if the English language is indeed the unlocking factor for a community's potential, then the establishment of the Tara Arts Group must be a hopeful pointer to the future of Asian theatre in Britain. Tara does not – even though the East African connections are strong – align itself with any particular Asian community. They work in English: a deliberate step since they reject what they regard as the backward-looking nature of much Asian theatre. For them, as young people brought up here and less inclined than their first-generation elders to accept the status quo, Britain and their place in it has to be the focus of their work. The result has been plays devised and written by the group (notably Jatinder Verma).

Tara still has a long way to go. In particular it still needs to find its place within what is misleadingly called 'the Asian community'. Reactions to their work have ranged from enthusiasm to fury at what has been regarded as deracinated and elitist. Radical Asian youth has criticized them in their open discussion forums for not dealing in an outright manner with racism in British society. Tara claims that that is not their aim. They believe that it is equally important that their communities in Britain recognize the strain of their situation and the double-think that it engenders. Despite criticism, their work is intelligent, incisive and theatrically promising.

It is interesting that, broadly speaking, Asian theatre is following a similar line of development to black theatre. A range of work is beginning to emerge — from the drawing-room comedies that assert the eternal verities of Indian values to the younger more questioning work (in the Bangladeshi groups as well as Tara). The element present in the black equation that is missing in the Asian is the outlet to the media. Very little work by Asian writers or dealing with Asian areas of life or involving Asian actors has reached the television screen or, indeed, beyond odd examples like *A Passage to India*, reached the mainstream theatre. There is no Asian equivalent to *Empire Road* (although we tried — unsuccessfully, for many reasons — in Hindi with *Parosi*). There is no Asian actor with the cross-the-board stature of Norman Beaton. But until there are more English-language drama groups like Tara, the actors and writers will not emerge to complete the equation.

References

1 Su Braden *Artists and People* (Routledge & Kegan Paul, 1978).
2 Lindsay Anderson *The Encore Reader* (Methuen, 1965).
3 Charles Marowitz *ibid.*
4 Norman Marshall *The Other Theatre* (John Lehmann, 1947).
5 Jenny Harris in an interview with the author.
6 From an interview with the author.
7 From an interview with the author.
8 Baz Kershaw *Theatre Quarterly* No. 30, Summer 1978.
9 Julian Hilton *Theatre Quarterly* No. 33, Spring 1979.
10 Telford Community Arts Annual Report, October 1978–September 1979.
11 Baz Kershaw *op. cit.*
12 From an interview with the author.
13 *ibid.*
14 Ed Berman in an interview with the author.

5 Agents of the Future

Theatre-in-Education

Tony Coult

Only up to the age of 17 or so does our fragmented culture accord any real seriousness and support to the process of learning, and much of its efforts then go to create social conformity. It is not surprising, then, that in the brief collision of national affluence and educational idealism in the early sixties, a new theatre form for young people should struggle into being, a form which has, over the intervening years, nourished much else in the Alternative Theatre.

Definitions of Theatre-in-Education are notoriously slippery. Circumstances of funding, of company history, of company policy all help to blur easy distinctions. That said, there are useful categorizations that can help. TIE is a theatre form performed by professionals, experienced and/or trained in both theatre and teaching technique. Companies usually work with one class per visit – say, a maximum of 40 young people – and companies perceive their work as, in some sense, educational.

The first team to use the label 'Theatre-in-Education' was formed in Coventry in 1965, the year that also saw the birth of CAST and The People Show. At that time it would have been difficult to conceive of the work as 'underground', in the way that CAST and People Show clearly were, coming as it did from the reasonably respectable modern marriage between the state education system and the predominantly middle-class repertory theatre. Yet this decent, liberal child of mid-sixties' idealism has become honed into what, at its best, is a clear-headed, sharp-witted dialectical theatre for young people – a true inheritor of Brecht's political aesthetics.

It was probably the 1944 Education Act, establishing free, compulsory schooling for all, that was most responsible for the sixties' liberalization of educational theory and practice. What was good for the individual took the place, gradually, of what was good for the Nation. In colleges of education, new ideas, formulated by theorists such as Piaget and Vygotsky, gave a sound basis of theory to child development, rooting it in the processes of socialization. If the child is made by its society, and is not determined by pre-ordained gifts and limitations, important implications follow – for society and for the teachers who find themselves, in effect, the shapers of future society. Concentrating at first on finding new, more stimulating ways to present the traditional curriculum, many teachers soon found themselves questioning the very nature of learning in schools itself. Old models of competitive skill – and rote-learning – were challenged by new models of problem-solving, mixed ability teaching, co-operative working and self-discovery. Children were to be encouraged to construct their own realities rather than having it imposed upon them by adults. As compulsory education for all affected many more working-class children, so too, more working-class teachers entered the profession, challenging the basic premises of education.

One effect of this liberalization process, kept bubbling by the prevailing affluence, was to push to the front of educational thought the technique of drama. As early as 1951, the basic principles of drama work in schools were being set out: "Dramatic work is of the utmost value in developing the children's grasp of reality. Children act things out in order to understand them".[1] Since the end of the war there had been a dedicated band of pioneers arguing for, and attempting to practise, theatre for children and theatre by children. The work of such as Peter Slade, Brian Way, and Caryl Jenner certainly held the ground for drama in the early post-war years. If now we look critically at their work, it is that the idealization of the child's 'naturalness' 'spontaneity' and 'creativity' tended to ignore the social nature of human experience. Individual development, self-exploration, introversion through the magic of theatre were the goals. It was something of a mirror-image of the wider theatre scene over which Christopher Fry presided, an idealistic, benign deity. It also represented the indulgent dead-end of the new thinking, and to some extent foreshadowed the dafter experiments of the middle and late sixties in social and educational practice.

From those beginnings, and encouraged by the establishment of Drama Advisers, theorists such as Gavin Bolton and Dorothy Heathcote began to develop drama-in-education into a formidable teaching tool. Their work emphasizes not vague 'creativity' but precise emotional and cognitive experience. Drama becomes a medium in which, through the playing-out of roles, the child can test her own experience, or models of experience. The implications of these models can be lived, and success or failure risked in a protected environment. The process is analogous to that of the less structured world of the playground. Drama is, ironically, the one practical teaching technique discovered by children and appropriated by teachers.

The other progenitor of what we now call TIE was the theatre. Again, the relative affluence of the late fifties had brought forth a number of new repertory theatres, responding to a renewal of bourgeois civic pride rather than to any obvious popular demand. The first new post-war repertory theatre was the Belgrade at Coventry, and its director was Tony Richardson. Together with Gordon Vallins, a teacher employed by the theatre to forge links with schools, he envisioned and brought into being the very first Theatre-in-Education team. It seems clear now that the establishment of a TIE team had as much to do with theatre policy towards the community (or simply theatre public relations) as to any clearly defined educational priorities. Its initial aims were defined by Gordon Vallins as: ". . . to explore the values of drama in the development of the child's personality, to experiment in teaching methods using drama and theatre techniques, and to stimulate an interest in theatre in adult life".[2]

The history of Theatre-in-Education can now be seen as its search for an adequate theoretical base. Some idea of the tentativeness and ex-perimental tone of the early days can be gained from Vallins' formulation. That kind of exploratory imprecision was, however, exactly what was wanted. It allowed the company to create its own patch, to define and refine the job as it worked. By 1968, when Stuart Bennett was team leader, the theoretical base was clearly firmer: "It was a company concerned with a theatre of ideas, simple and imaginative, which communicated directly in classroom or school hall – our first priority was relating to the child in his own environment".[3]

Companies were still tending to work primarily with drama teachers in schools, and their novel input was perceived as inspirational, stimulating, galvanic, even perhaps a little anarchic. It took time for teachers to become clear what they were being offered and time for actor/teachers to realize *why* they were being so successful. As the movement spread – to Bolton, Leeds, London, the fringe theatre of the late sixties was developing and feeding in its own energies to the educational debate. Ed Berman's pioneering work on games and participatory street theatre took ideas about learning which were at the heart of TIE technique and applied them to a wide range of social situations, including youth clubs, playgrounds, mental hospitals and adult community centres. Albert Hunt's experi-mentation with theatre as a learning tool at Bradford Art College, and the growing use of a didactic (i.e. 'teaching') style of agitprop by groups such as CAST and Red Ladder, began to demolish the barriers between education and entertainment, between private and public learning.

The new breed of 'actor/teacher' (the specially coined term indicating two whole skills united rather than two half-skills awkwardly married) were as likely to come from colleges of education or universities, as from the drama schools. They were likely, therefore, to demand an intellectual framework to the work, where the vocationally trained actor might be content with his skills in the cattle-market of professional theatre. This demand for a theoretical basis to their work implied an inevitable quickening of the political consciousness and this tied in with the greater proportion of working-class TIE workers. (TIE has recently become aware of the need to match the theoretical level of the work with theatre craft skill, a baby which has sometimes been thrown out with the bathwater).

By the early seventies this raised political consciousness amongst TIE workers expressed itself in several ways. The use of Drama in Education to help the child understand her social environment soon implied shows which focused on particular issues with strong political implications. The left and libertarian-leaning nature of most companies found itself alerted by the election of the Heath government in 1970, and by the subsequent miners' strike. This confrontation with the working class, whose sons and daughters formed the great bulk of TIE's audiences, raised the political temperature and caused many TIE practitioners to re-think their role. The old, somehow cosy ideas of galvanizing the teaching situation, of helping the child to adjust to the world, began to look either inadequate (galvanize the teaching to what end?) or even reactionary (why help the child to adjust to a world which is unjust and irrational?). It became important for many teams to perform programmes that brought children to a clearer understanding of class and industrial politics. In their own union, Equity, actor/teachers, perhaps less prone to the reactionary mystiques of conventional market-place theatre, were active in the Fight for a Living Wage for actors, and in the call for a Branch and Delegate structure. The TIE contract negotiated by Equity is still the least bad of all its contracts.

By 1972 the burgeoning TIE movement was gaining self-consciousness, which was expressed in the formation of the Standing Conference of Young People's Theatre, embracing as well as the TIE companies who worked within the state education system, others who performed theatre in community venues, youth clubs and playgrounds. The annual SCYPT Conferences became the focus for vigorous, often painful, debate between companies about what work they should do, and how they should do it. At the 1974 Conference in Aberystwyth, much energy was spent on the issue of company organization, and the expressed desire of so many companies to work collectively marked an important step in the movement's development. As democrats in politics, most team members strove for some kind of democratic decision-making anyway and it was normal for work to be collectively devised, but formally structuring democratic working was far trickier. Theatre boards and Local Education Authorities like individuals to deal with, and some TIE directors found it difficult to devolve power to other team members. By the same token, teams with no tradition of self-management found it difficult to reconcile efficiency and coherence of policy with democracy.

By 1979 SCYPT was performing a valuable service to the movement as a whole but it had also got itself diverted into a cul-de-sac with the appointment of a professional officer to raise funds and represent the movement to the outside world. As SCYPT was unable to agree on a global policy for the officer to carry out, that model for its future folded, and was replaced in 1979 with an alternative model – a forum for debate, criticism and sharing of experience aimed at the raising of standards in all departments.

The 1979 Conference at Essex University took as its title *Theatre, Education and Politics* and set out to begin a broad theoretical debate about the work. Some fifteen years on from its origins, the older members of the movement were obviously feeling a need to question what they were doing. Newcomers to the work can no longer feel that they are entering a new, pioneering field, and they too need criteria and theory, to be equipped to make the critical judgements necessary to create TIE in the straitened circumstances of the eighties. SCYPT now attempts to answer this need.

Before looking at the position of TIE now, it would be well to look at the TIE experience itself. As it exists in the non-public venues of school halls and classrooms, the number of people, apart from young audiences, who have seen the work, is small, and a surprising number of well-informed commentators on Alternative Theatre still don't know what actually goes on in a TIE programme! TIE's characteristic formal device, and an actual innovation in theatre technique, is some form of active participation by the audience. There is a whole spectrum of degree and effectiveness of participation, from a discussion following straight theatre display through to engineered situations which, to the child, are indistinguishable from 'real life'. The function of participation will be to allow each member of the class to experience a dramatic situation set up by the actors, to make judgements and take action within the dramatic situation, and to experience the consequences of those judgements. The particular form of participation chosen will depend on the age-group, the size of class, the content of the programme, and on the traditions and collective experience of the company.

One form of participation which combines clear drama teaching techniques with theatre display and dramatic structure is represented by the Coventry team's 1978 programme *The Price of Coal*. A class is drawn into involvement and identification with opposing characters or ideas. The conflict of interest will be experienced in the acting-out, with children acting themselves, in a dramatic situation set up by TIE actors playing characters. In *The Price of Coal* an actor goes into a classroom playing a modern coal-miner to talk about mining in the seventeenth century, he takes off his modern overalls and helmet, and is seen to be dressed underneath as a seventeenth-century miner.

Now the class is split into two groups and each group learns, with a 'miner', the two different techniques of mining employed by Warwickshire and Staffordshire miners. Each group mimes the hacking of the coal, the discipline of listening for danger signals, and for the tell-tale creaking which might presage a roof-fall. The mimed work is energetic and disciplined, and commits the child physically to the action. In the school

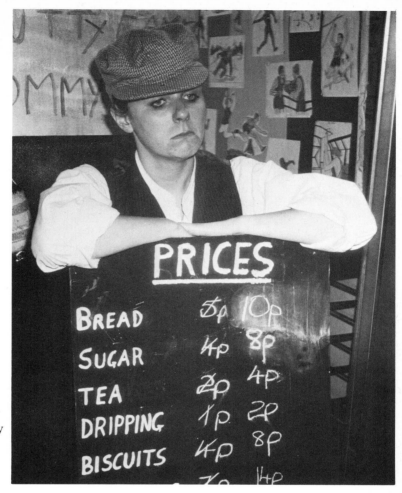

The Coventry Theatre-in-Education team's project *The Price of Coal* for Junior schoolchildren analyses the economic conditions of miners in the seventeenth century. The Coventry company was the first TIE group to be established in Britain.

hall, two 'mines' – black canvas-covered tunnels – have been set up. Here each group works, in hot, dark and cramped conditions, experiencing some discomfort and alert for the (taped) sounds of danger. As the programme proceeds the children absorb the social and historical detail through the play. Eventually they meet the owner of the mines, Lord Newdigate, who brings the two groups into competition. He wants the most productive technique possible, takes on the Staffordshire miners and sacks the rest. The rejected group responds by working harder; they ignore safety warnings, and finally narrowly escape a 'roof-fall'. One of their number, the actor miner, is killed. The dynamics, the class relationships and the results of competitive capitalism in the seventeenth century are thus vividly taught with great emotional clarity to the whole class.

The form of *The Price of Coal* is one common at Junior level, mixing drama teaching techniques such as occupational mime, and theatre display. Many teams have explored the participation spectrum on either side of that form, however. The play with no (or very little) involvement other than as audience by the class, has made something of a resurgence in TIE lately, as teams become more skilled in traditional theatre technique and recognize its potential for offering theatre images which help to clarify ideas and objectify experience. The Minimata mercury poisoning scandal was dramatized by the Coventry team in *Drink The Mercury* using a version of the very formal techniques of Japanese theatre – a narrator, an actor impersonating the chemical factory with a mask, different coloured sashes for different characters, etc. In that this was a Junior programme, it was perhaps exceptional, as 'pure' theatre is usually performed for secondary groups. Examples would be Cockpit TIE's *Marches* about the rise of Fascism in the thirties and *Ways of Change*, about the English Revolution in the seventeenth century. (Both these programmes, however, were preceded by half-day workshops in which the students seeing the programme worked with the characters in the play in open-ended discussion and improvisation sessions.)

At another extreme, at which theatre display appears to play a very small part, comes a programme like Perspectives Theatre Company's 1979 *Spaces*. This was primarily a programme for infants about the physical properties of objects. At its most superficial level it could be taken to teach simple concepts such as tessellation, colour, shape, texture, weight and so on. However, it was devised after a study of the work of Edward de Bono, and his analytical and teaching methods were built in from the start. The four actor/teachers were simply a team of inventors with 'Inventing Kits' – collections of shapes of unusual shape, texture, weight, etc. They were there to ask the class's help in investigating the physical properties of the shapes. In a free-play session three groups did just this. The actor/teacher's job was to listen but not to judge, to provoke continued questioning and experimenting but not to offer solutions. Half-way through the programme the Inventors' team leader asked the class to invent either a sleep-inducing machine, an animal trap or an explorer's raft, using the shapes as building-blocks, endowed with whatever properties they wished. Moving now from the individual discovery of the first session to the group work of the second stretched each child considerably. Their vocabulary and use of language to convey concepts was also continually tested in discussion with the Inventors and with each other. Although very few conventional theatre techniques were used, there was still a conscious use of dramatic structure, with theatre design (more precisely, Theatre-in-Education design) and role-play contributing the greater part of the theatre experience. Nonetheless, in encouraging children to investigate material reality through play, to make decisions and to structure their own solutions to problems, *Spaces* followed the underlying principles of most Theatre-in-Education.

TIE programmes typically last for half a day, but having a whole day, more ambitious projects can be undertaken. The Greenwich TIE team's *Race Against Time* was a whole day programme which took three different approaches. In the morning a role-play simulation game was played in which school students and actors together recreate the experience of immigrants arriving in the country. Some students become 'native' inhabitants of a new town, others 'immigrant' workers from a former colony. At first all people in the town benefit and accrue the material rewards of income and housing deemed appropriate for their class and occupation. As the economic situation in the new town deteriorates, however, the immigrants find themselves being increasingly blamed for the troubles which beset everyone, not least themselves. At the same time immigration laws change and the immigrant group finds it increasingly difficult to become re-united with their families still waiting to join them. As pressures mount, spokesmen for the different groups begin to emerge, and finally a meeting is called to unravel the web of rumours, accusations and misunderstandings that has built up. By comparing their experiences during the game the pupils are able to see how the situation has occurred and how the 'immigrants' have been blamed for problems which have very different causes.

In the afternoon the same students watch a play about the circumstances

'Spaces' Inventing Kit – a de Bono-based programme devised by the Perspectives TIE Company.

surrounding the murder of a West Indian youth. The final session of the programme allows pupils to work in small groups with characters from the play and the morning's simulation.

The very full involvement in school life implied by such a whole day visit as *Race Against Time* symbolizes something of the relationship teams have with teachers. Most teams have a formal link with teachers in the form of some kind of advisory board, but whatever the precise relationship, TIE teams try to work as specialized inputs into a programme of teaching, consulting with teachers prior to the visit in the devising process, and offering a teaching pack and suggestions for follow-up work.

None of the programmes detailed here is necessarily representative of TIE, other than indicating its variety. However, in the broad aims and solutions they offer, they share certain features. In the eighties, then, what can we say characterizes TIE? These are propositions which I think most TIE workers would subscribe to:

1 TIE sets out to explain the processes of the material world. Those processes may be physical (e.g. a programme like *Spaces*), or historical and social (e.g. *The Price of Coal* and *Race Against Time*).
2 TIE uses the symbolic language of theatre to describe these processes, because theatre art makes abstract ideas concrete and personal.
3 TIE places great emphasis on the involvement of its audience in the world of the play, because it seeks to encourage them to construct their own meaning from the evidence the play provides.
4 TIE seeks to nurture creative, sceptical and analytical systems of thought in young people.
5 TIE is a humanistic art-form. It supposes that human nature is not fixed or universal, but is determined by social activity, and is therefore alterable.

As more workers in TIE take stock of their work, the need for some acceptable theoretical base to tie together such vague propositions as these now seems paramount. Theories of education, theories of theatre practice and aesthetic theories, need to be found which fertilize each other and give coherence to the work. A 'common sense' theory of TIE needs to be established. Some companies have begun to study dialectical materialism as the only theory of knowledge adequate to the educational process in a scientific age. They are committing themselves to a continuing process of political analysis and education, offering, through their work not the fuel for revolution, but some of the 'social imagination' (in Enzensberger's phrase) with which the educationally starved young working class can structure understanding of the mystified and covert workings of the social world.

These intentions and the methods of approaching the work outlined above may seem to sit uneasily with the accepted versions of children's art and entertainment that most of us grew up with. But that is only evidence of the fragmented way our society manipulates its young, who deserve and demand the same pleasures of understanding as adults. Another fragmentation is the very isolation of TIE itself from other branches of alternative theatre. Despite the fact that many TIE workers move into the fringe (often because the financial restraints in TIE companies inhibit the possibilities for a proper development of their craft), TIE still seems to sit to one side of alternative theatre as a whole. It is perhaps perceived as regional, small-scale, only 'half-theatre'. Nonetheless, what is remarkable about the present situation is the growing together of the aims of different kinds of theatre work. Consider this statement about dramatic method:

> "The 'dramatization of the analysis instead of the story', in both the choice and ordering of the scenes and in the incidents dramatically emphasized in the scenes, is a way of reinstating meaning in literature. It may seem cold and abstract but it is not. The analysis can give us the beauty and vitality that once belonged to myth, without its compromises and intellectual reallocation of meaning. [These dramatizations] demonstrate those crises in a story when the audience are asked to be not passive victims or witnesses, but interpreters of experience, agents of the future, restoring meaning to action by recreating self-consciousness. At these moments, the audience are superior to the actors: they are on the real stage".[4]

That is a playwright, Edward Bond, with no direct experience of TIE work, yet analysing dramatic method in terms that will be almost second nature to the creators of TIE.

The eighties pose difficult questions for all alternative theatre. TIE is a branch of community theatre that cannot survive without substantial subsidy, and we must face the fact that it is threatened with virtual extinction. The Arts Council no longer acknowledges any responsibility for sustaining it, while local authorities are often ill-informed of the TIE method and are in any case far more liable to reactionary pressure to cut out 'frills' (sic). It is clear that a greater clarity of vision of the role of all art is going to be necessary for any form of popular art to survive. Creating 'agents of the future' is one of TIE's goals but it is increasingly clear that it is a goal to be shared by all of the alternative theatre.

References

1 City of Aberdeen Education Committee *The Curriculum of the Primary School*, quoted in *Drama in Education: The Annual Survey No. 1*, p. 93, edited by John Hodgson and Martin Bantam (Pitman, 1972).
2 *ibid.* p. 104.
3 Stuart Bennett *Rare Earth* (Eyre Methuen, 1976).
4 Edward Bond 'A Note on Dramatic Method' in *The Bundle* (Eyre Methuen, 1978).

6 The Arena of Exploration
Children's theatre

Rosalind Asquith

"The aim . . . would be to place theatre in its true position, as
a catalyst, an arena, in which the values of civilization are
explored, human experience is tested. In short, where the
world of the child is enriched by theatre art, and not where
the art is seen as an extension of child-minding."[1]

Traditionally proclaiming its solidarity with W. C. Fields' observation that
anyone who hates dogs and children can't be all bad, the British Theatre
establishment ignores the possibility that children could be paying customers (except, of course, at pantomime whose roots already lie in popular
theatre) and tends to represent them on stage in a manner so cloyingly
patronizing that even the young Shirley Temple would blush. Not surprisingly the consensus of theatrical opinion about children's theatre veers
between commiseration (a view that assumes that no actor in his/her right
sense would get involved in such demeaning work except for reasons of
sheer survival) and a whimsical sentimentality that sees in the 'magic of
the stage' an endlessly diverting world for the little ones.

It is hardly surprising that even the well-intentioned are ignorant of
children's theatre. The Arts Council's Working Party that reported on the
subject in 1978 is still the only serious investigation of the area currently
available, although even that, at the time of writing, remains unpublished.
Very few people in our resolutely paternalistic society take the trouble to
find out what children actually *want* (and this is one of the principal
reasons why traditional children's theatre is frequently so poor) but over
the past fifteen years or so a considerable number of theatre companies
have devoted their energies to the idea that children's theatre is an art in
its own right – as audacious, humane, illuminating, humorous and dis-
concerting as any other.

There are now some sixty professional groups working for children, of
which roughly a quarter, such as the Durham Children's Theatre and
London's Unicorn Theatre, specialize in children's theatre, while the rest
are community theatre groups with policies which include specialist work
for children, Dance in Education companies and puppet groups. (Though

only in Britain would the assumption be made that all puppet theatre is theatre for children.) In addition, there are over thirty Theatre-in-Education and Young People's Theatre Groups attached to regional theatres; schemes such as the Young People's Theatre Scheme at the Royal Court designed to encourage writing and performance by children; and a handful of Local Education Authority groups. However, nearly a quarter of all these outfits are London-based. So, despite all the post-war beavering away by educationalists about stimulation of the youthful imagination and about learning through creative activity, the theatre groups working specifically for children are obliged to survive on shoestring budgets, and all the laudable affirmations stand in the shadow of one depressing statistic: less than 50% of Britain's children between the ages of five and fourteen see even one live theatrical performance a year.[2]

Though local authorities had occasionally financed theatre work for children (generally in the form of presenting classical plays in schools) since the 1944 Education Act, children's theatre remained a peripheral activity until the late sixties. Like the burgeoning fringe, it grew out of a response to the deficiencies of the established theatre which was seen as a privileged form of leisure activity for middle-class adult audiences. At the same time came the implementation of progressive educational theories which argued a direct connection between learning and creative activity. Children's theatre became a bridge between the play of children and the play of theatre.

Theatre is the mimetic representation of action: it mirrors life. Children's play is permeated with mimetic modes of behaviour. (And, unlike traditional children's theatre, children do not confine themselves to imitating people – windmills, trains, animals, spirits, machinery of all kinds are grist to the child's imaginative mill.) Humanity's capacity for seeing resemblances is shown in the earliest proto-drama: the ritual cultic dances imitated the progress of the stars with the express purpose of manipulating such similarity so that the stars would follow a favourable course. The mimetic genius is, thus, a life-determining force.

Modern adults see in the world only the minimal residues of the magical correspondences and analogies familiar to ancient peoples. And modern industrial society determines precisely the roles each adult must play: mother/father, wife/husband, 'housewife'/worker. For children the world is still magical and learning is precisely the testing of many different behavioural roles.

For adults who go to the theatre as passive spectators the display of actors becoming the characters they portray is sufficient release. For children, who perceive in the actors' mimetic behaviour something deeply familiar, passive spectating is not nearly enough: thus the hallmark of children's theatre is audience participation. The bond between stage and audience in children's theatre is not that of shared experience but of a shared activity (mimetic behaviour) which in the adult world is either tabooed or marginalized. The position of audiences in adult theatre is as consumer and critic; in children's theatre it is as fan and technician.

Not only do children demand higher standards of performance from that of adult professional presentations, but children's theatre is, accordingly, a unique field which demands different skills and experience. Like all skills, however, these can be learned: for instance, young children tend not to understand irony and are likely to mistake seriousness for threat. At a more technical level, conventions of adult theatre can create the opposite effect for children. Thus blacking out the stage releases the tension of a climax for adults whereas it tends to leave children feeling abandoned and confused. But any genre of adult theatre can be adapted for presentation to children, whether tragedy, comedy, slapstick, or politically or socially aware plays. This in part explains the great variety within children's theatre, which is limited only by the lack of life experience of its young audiences.

London's Unicorn Theatre – an exception to the generally itinerant character of children's theatre groups – was, in fact, established in 1948 by the late Caryl Jenner though it only moved to the Arts Theatre in the West End in 1967. The Unicorn, which in part fulfills Jenner's dream of a National Children's Theatre, has hosted a number of the recent developments in children's theatre that best embody the vision of a ". . . world of the child . . . enriched by theatre art".[3]

Ken Campbell – a virtuoso of the absurd – is uncannily sensitive to the imaginative delight children take in the logic of nonsense and their ability to manufacture a vocabulary which describes what, for them, are some of the serious issues of the world. 'Jimjamjammering', for instance, means spreading strawberry jam on your pyjamas; 'pranicking' describes the action of picking yourself up by the seat of your pants. His *Old King Cole*, rejigged for the Unicorn under the title *Paraphernalia*, contained some startling comic performances, notably Matyelok Gibbs' clownish interpretation of Twoo, partner to magician Faz, specialist in traps and disguises. Harpo-like they would produce inexhaustible supplies of sausages from the innermost depths of their garments, proferring them cigarette-like with the solicitous enquiry "Do you sausage?".

Audience participation has been seen at its most exhilatory at the Unicorn far outstripping the weary 'oh yes he did' routines of the Christmas pantomime. Ken Whitmore's *Jump* (1976), for example, demands complete collaboration from its audience in its finale: the entire gathering must jump in the air to save the world. (Bewilderingly, *Jump* was first heard on late night radio!) Whitmore's play represents the best approach to structured children's theatre: it is witty, densely written and covers a complex of social issues – science, TV, politics – with an open but sophisticated blend of satire and sobriety.

Things That Go Bump in the Night presented in 1979 at the Unicorn, one of London's longest established children's theatres.

However, perhaps the most encouraging success to date at the Unicorn has been *Things that Go Bump in the Night*, a translation by Roy Kift of a play originally performed by the German children's theatre group Gripps. Dealing primarily with fear (of the dark, of being left alone) it also excels in treating more 'sensitive' subjects such as child-beating, one-parent families, toy guns and TV advertising. It is packed with insight and fun, avoids dull polemic, treats a single mother with genuine sympathy and portrays a little girl as somewhat wiser and more adventurous than her elder brother.

As yet there is no theatre company emerging in Britain of the stature and considered convictions of Gripps, though much progress has been made over the past few years. Thus the conventionally structured community group, Common Stock – which bases most of its work on improvisations, discussions and workshops with local children – invades the highly charged territory of sex role stereotyping. Common Stock has consistently mounted plays for children of the sort of idiosyncratic, challenging and unpatronizing kind that writers on the fringe are well placed to produce but which most of the media is disposed to ignore. Frank Whitten's *Morning Tiger*, for instance, combined compassionate social comment with a high level of excitement. It was situated in two places: the planet Exox (whose limbless tubular woolly inhabitants are clearly ex-socks), and Dickensian London. Various inventive forms of villainy punctuate the action: on Earth a murdering circus manager holds captive the title's hero – half boy, half tiger, while on Exox a vacuum-like Mind Eater is at large, capable of swallowing thoughts and therefore of defying attempts to outwit it. Common Stock's play is a pertinent example of a work that would warrant some celebration by any theatrical standards and proof that workshops and discussions with children provide fertile ground. Its complexity of structure and imagination may be the reverse, theatrically, of the fine detailing and psychological analysis of naturalism but it is by no means inferior.

As anarchic and eccentric as the Ken Campbell Roadshow and working in a rather similar tradition as travelling players, the Cornish Footsbarn group virtually defines the divide between the routine and humdrum commercial children's theatre and the work that is done on the fringe. Typically, they rework the conventional repertoire of young people's plays though the results are often highly idiosyncratic and not at all stereotyped. Their 1978 version of *Robin Hood* – a story done to death in a hundred unimaginative versions in theatre, film and television – included a bizarre, babbling three-headed Sheriff of Nottingham, a virtuoso musi-

Common Stock at the Unicorn in *Tales From Whitechapel*. This sequence is *Daniel's Story*, written by 9-year-old Daniel Henry about the haves and the have-nots.

cian Alan a'Dale and an athletic sword-fighting Maid Marian. Footsbarn work in the open as well as in village halls, for adults as well as children. With their spin-off group for younger children, The Barnies, they have overwhelming local support. Perhaps partly because of the security of this local rapport and because of the distance from London, they have developed into one of the most outstanding children's groups in Britain.

Groups like Footsbarn and Common Stock, however, tend to be the exception not the rule. Though there are children's plays by Dickens, Dylan Thomas, John Arden and Margaretta D'Arcy, Barrie Keeffe, and – naturally enough – adaptations of stories by Hans Christian Andersen and of Louisa M. Alcott's *Little Women*, much material has gone untapped. Meanwhile, the material used reflects both the prevalent male bias (the ratio of male to female roles in children's plays is well over two to one[4]) and the attitude that sees children as second-class citizens. A recent report noted that ". . . of the programmes seen, about half of those available to infants were considered to underestimate the imaginative and intellectual abilities of children".[5] This survey is backed up by the personal observations of Nick Barter, the present artistic director of the Unicorn. His conclusion is that lack of imagination in children's theatre has acquired an inexorable momentum: theatre directors and writers are subconsciously fixated on the cliches they saw themselves as children and simply reproduce them.

A case in point here is David Wood, whose commercial success with plays like the musical *The Gingerbread Man* has led him to be dubbed 'National Children's Playwright'. Wood has made an impressive effort to write accessible and unpatronizing plays for the junior and primary age-groups, using a good many orthodox pantomime participatory devices but stretching the expectations with unusual settings and characters. Thus *The Gingerbread Man* is set on a kitchen dresser. Its world is one where sugar cubes are as big as building blocks and teapots as large as cottages; and amongst the inhabitants are the salt and pepper pots (a rare opportunity for a star part for a black actress) and a nasty old bag (tea, of course) who lives on the top shelf. However, the plot – which centres around Herr von Cuckoo, who loses his voice and is threatened with the dustbin – hinges on simple suspense and seems fairly unadventurous when set against much of the work of the Unicorn, Common Stock or Footsbarn.

On the other hand, another of Wood's plays shows that he is prone to unconsidered reflection of adult stereotypes. *Plotters of Cabbage Patch Corner*, the first production of Wood's own company Whirligig, seems like the metaphorical equivalent of a leader in the *Daily Express*: its story hinges on the actions of some particularly unattractive and maggotty insects, who threaten to strike and ruin the garden.

Nevertheless, Wood's commitment to children's work must be applauded, particularly when contrasted with the marketing stratagems of most theatres. There is no reason why Michael Bogdanov's exemplary adaptations of classics such as *Hiawatha* and *The Ancient Mariner* at the National Theatre and the Young Vic could not have been programmed as part of the normal repertoire of those theatres. Their presentation over Christmas merely heightens the suspicion that those companies pay only lip-service to the concept and importance of children's theatre.

In theatre, motives and organization cannot be divorced from the end-product, and this is reflected in the very different children's shows presented by the likes of Footsbarn, Common Stock and a number of other 'fringe' groups on the one hand and the commercial and bourgeois theatre on the other. This difference is, perhaps, most particularly evident in those companies which specialize in presenting children's theatre in the open. Of course in some respects the circumstances in which such companies work enable them to tap the audience's enthusiasm for getting involved more extensively than in the constraining atmosphere of a theatre. This shouldn't detract, however from the radical and impressive work of companies like, for instance, Inter-Action's Dogg's Troupe, an innovative street-theatre gang who unleashed a thoroughly demystified brand of theatrical experience on the unsuspecting streets of Kentish Town in the early seventies.

Typical of the best of Inter-Action's way of working was sculptress Liz Leyh's project *Make A Circus*. In this, five or six members of the troupe dressed up as clowns, ring masters, and general circus hangers-on. Beating drums, wheeling cartfuls of old clothes, paper and assorted junk, and armed with megaphones, they invited any children in the vicinity to join in. A startling pied-piper effect soon turned a trickle of curious passers-by into a parade which was led into a park or playspace where the children would gather round a makeshift ring to watch a circus performance by the group. Afterwards the children were encouraged to perform their own circus – this could involve such improvised props and menagerie as a distinctly human-looking lion jumping through a hoop comprising two twelve-year-olds.

Drawing out the children's expressiveness while keeping the event as spontaneous as possible was only feasible with the high degree of skills possessed by the Dogg's Troupe. Such skills are often disputed, and the work categorized as more social work than theatre, by the more theatrically conventional. However, such comments only reflect the difference between the non-participatory adult theatre dominant in Britain (and, indeed, most of the Western world) and children's theatre which unites the two disparate meanings of 'play' into a shared, mimetic, activity.

In 1967 the Arts Council made its first specific allocation of subsidy (£90,000) to children's theatre, and the Young People's Theatre Panel was established. Funds were earmarked specifically for work for children. Seven years later this latter provision was dropped on the assumption that the movement had worked up sufficient momentum and therefore did not require such insurance any longer. However, all the evidence points to the fact that positive discrimination is essential to a Cinderella activity like children's theatre. In the period since 1974 the proportion of grants that regional repertory theatres have invested in children's theatre has gone down.[6] With the decision about investment restored to the artistic directors of those theatres, the tendency has been to re-distribute their grants at the expense of children's theatre. This tendency reflects not only the

Inter-Action's Fun Art Bus playing to the bus queues during the Festival of London, 1972.

epithet that the rich get richer and the poor poorer – a tendency all too well substantiated in the reality of modern Britain – but that the pressures on artistic directors from local councillors on the one hand and critics on the other force them to choose programmes which reflect their tastes for either 'popular' or 'artistic' productions.

Since children don't have the power of choice (and very little opportunity to vote with their feet at bad performances) it is up to adults to guard and develop the standards of children's theatre. Children are only completely absorbed and entertained by work that is coherent in its conception, sophisticated in its craft-skills (performance, design, direction) and realistic in the establishment of a relationship between the audience and the practitioners. Despite the inadequacy of the drama schools' preparation of actors for work in the field (a significant minority provide no special training at all[7]) and despite the low status of children's theatre within the profession and the feeling among actors that 'there are no Hamlets' to be found in it, there is an ever-growing number of groups attempting to take their theatrical responsibilities seriously. The assumption that all the old chestnuts simply need warming over for young audiences will survive as long as the profession and those who subsidize it choose not to recognize that the passivity with which children experience the second-rate is a sign of their own status as a captive audience rather than their contentment with it. Once they have seen the best they can tell that a diet of clapped-out plots, stereotyped confrontations and tacky magic stunts that work better on TV is selling their expectations short. Children love live theatre and their demands of it are much higher than those they make of film, which they know gets its effects through all manner of technical trickery. An acceptance among the very young that theatre is a place for fascination, wonder, challenge, can only be to the theatre's good in generations to come.

But despite its low status, the range of new initiatives (only a few of which have been outlined here) urges a note of cautious optimism for the future of children's theatre. As the Arts Council's Working Party commented: "Good relevant children's theatre in the seventies has faced social responsibility in the same terms as good adult theatre. Its world is not permanently sealed off in stories of the past and fantasies of the future."[8]

References

1 The Children's Theatre Working Party's Report to The Arts Council,
        1977–78.
2 *ibid.*
3 *The Bibliography of Selected Plays for Performance to and by
        Children* (The National Association for Drama in Education
        and Children's Theatre, 1979).
4 *Actors in Schools*, Department of Education and Science, Survey 22.
5, 6, 7, 8 As 1 above.

7 The Jazz of Dreams

Performance art

John Ashford

This chapter is about that vague area known as 'Performance Art' and since it *is* a vague area it should attempt to begin with a definition. Unfortunately there must be as many definitions of performance art as there are performance artists.

At one end of this individually painted spectrum are those who seek personally to realize a conceptual piece – American Anna Banana roller-skating around the world delivering telegrams of municipal greeting, or those like Stuart Brisley whose gallery installations often demand the physical presence of the artist. At the opposite end are conventionally trained actors who find themselves edging along the narrow springboard towards performance provided within a script by Jeff Nuttall, say, or by David Gale for Lumiere & Son. The ground in between might well include many who actually reject the term performance art; but it certainly must include the work of The People Show and the Welfare State, and of all those artists who have associated with either company at any time. In short, it must include performance which plays upon the expectations of theatre, which is a collaborative compilation, without any one writer, director or designer, and the substance of which is the unpredictable but structured interplay of sound, object and action.

Any attempt at definition must be pragmatic since (unlike in Poland) there is little discussion of theory in Britain – this is neither a 'school' nor a discipline to be learned. Performance art constantly re-defines itself according to the work presented: there are no rules.

If the work refuses to be pinned down then it is this volatile nature which keeps it at the forefront of experiment in British theatre. It is also that elusiveness which makes it difficult to write about, additionally complicated by the proposition that if there's one thing performance work is *not* about, it's words. Most critics who have a go are usually reduced to mere description. Some admit to an emotional response but fail to analyse what has evoked it. National newspaper critics, faced with a theatrical artefact which relies neither on plot nor character in the usual sense, have largely given up – if they ever bothered to make an attempt in the first

Left: Mark Long of The People Show. With over 80 different shows in 15 years, The People Show are undoubtedly the most prolific and creative performance art group. They are the post-Dadaists of British theatre, while their shows – collages of atmospheres and moods structured around a theme – have a staggering range: anarchic, lyrical, fantastical, autumnal, menacing, savagely comic and possessed of a cool, self-distancing irony.

Right: José Nava of The People Show: "My generation shares an idea that the theatre not only describes but actually shows new possibilities." – Howard Brenton.

Below: Landscapes and Living Spaces – Roland and Shirley. Roland Miller (formerly with The People Show) and Shirley Cameron typically disturb every-day reality, often in a light-hearted way.

place. It is sad and damaging that the work which is at the forefront of experiment is the least publicly discussed.

But there is good reason for this failure, the failure to develop a critical language with which to approach performance work. Our theatre is heavily literary and there is still the vestige of an academic tradition which upholds that a great play can be better appreciated in the study than on the stage. Our criticism mirrors this preoccupation. We know little of the non-literary European traditions of commedia, of mime, of cabaret or circus. Perhaps the British relative of that tradition survived in music-hall; but this area of performance has been accorded critical status only in retrospect and only after artists like Buster Keaton have worked with Beckett, and Max Wall has brought his carefully honed performance personality to the 'straight' stage. This division between 'straight', respectable theatre and popular entertainment has left the British critic without a basic approach to work which is not necessarily about *what* is done but about *the way* that it is done.

The British insistence on the supremacy of the text also tends to literally blinker the critic when he enters the theatre. The visual image is seen as secondary to the main business of the evening, an optional extra for support and clarification. Indeed, this is often true, and rightly so, for that is the nature of the work. Now and again our theatre is galvanized by the visit of a company from abroad who naturally express themselves in a forceful marriage of word and image, and the critics applaud. But when the visual image is at the centre of the stage as in performance work, the critic has learned to keep away for he has no experience of coping with the nature of the presentation. The problem for him here is that the image is not used symbolically but for its own sake. The accumulation of images can have an emotional effect but no single meaning is proposed. For the art critic, of course, this is nothing new: it is his stock in trade. For the theatre critic, however, it seems to attack his perceived role at the root. Surely it is his job to extrapolate meaning and to assess the success of its public communication. Here he is faced with work which is obsessively personal, that means something different to each of its performers, and something different to every member of its audience, and probably many different things again the following night. The single basis of objective, detached evaluation is clearly no longer sufficient. What is he to do?

At this point it would be good to answer the question, to spell out a new critical vocabulary. But it is not possible. In the true spirit of performance work each commentator must find his own solution. And by the combination of such responses, a language by which we can talk about performance art should develop. This may not necessarily be of any use to the work for it will continue to resist the approach of any academic discipline. But it would help create a better informed and wider-based audience; and it is for this reason that responsible critical reaction is crucial.

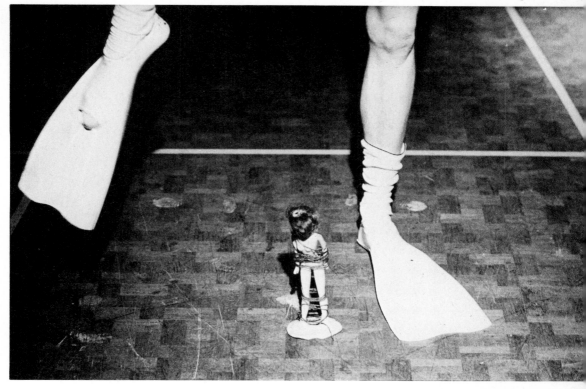

The Yorkshire-based John Bull Puncture Repair Kit was an anarchic early seventies combo composed variously of Diz Willis, George O'Brien, Al Beach, Mick Banks and Ian Hinchcliffe. Their speciality was madness and comedy: "We have a script of sorts but not the closely annotated, verbal sort, more a running order or workplan, with cues and clearly defined points in it for innovation and improvisation. (When he has strangled the last cat we burst into song – after the blackout we drag steam-rollers around with our teeth. No gags, keep it frightening.)" – Diz Willis, 1975.

Performance art is generally held by the uninitiated to be obscure, difficult, endemically of minority appeal. It isn't. Despite critical silence it has developed a committed audience. With sympathetic critical encouragement, that audience would grow – for everyone has dreams, and of all contemporary theatre, performance art is the stuff of dreams.

What is appropriate here is an indication of some of the aesthetic concerns of the sixties and seventies which lead artists towards performance work, a sort of relief map in the absence of a body of responsible criticism. Performance artists tend to develop from a fine art tradition, so the first five markers are in that area.

First: an emphasis on process rather than product. This concern currently runs through many different disciplines in emulation of the freedom of the improvising jazz musician. It's an age-old principle

Left: Welfare State – 'the Lords of Misrule' – on the streets of Burnley, Lancashire, where they were based for some years during the mid-seventies. Since then they have worked in various localities, generally in the North of England.

Below: Welfare State in *Uppendown Mooney* in Liverpool, 1978. Though usually classified as performance artists with a forte for blending myth, ritual, rock and visual image, the State has continually crossed the critical demarcation lines, often working over days or weeks within defined communities where they systematically plant images and ideas and demonstrate a process encouraging local people to make their own artistic celebrations.

and yet conventional actors are still known to criticize The People Show for asking the public to pay to see rehearsals. In the same way, conventional dancers accuse contemporary dancers of presenting warm-up exercises in lieu of finished choreography. Performance art grows directly from the notion that the act of creation is of greater significance than the thing created.

Second: a rejection of the art commodity market. A performance cannot become an artefact bought and sold for profit. The artist's physical presence places the work under his complete control and emphasizes his place within and interaction with society. Artists present work free in public spaces. The everyday environment itself becomes the art object when re-focused by an action of the artist, however minimal.

Third: an interest in kinetic sculpture. If sculpture is to move then the artist's most immediate material is his own body.

Fourth: a renewed interest in Dada, particularly that work to do with collage and the juxtaposition of apparently unrelated images.

Fifth: a new concern with the process by which a found object becomes a work of art. A car tyre in a gallery draws attention to itself as a sculptural form, to the intricacy of the moulding and the way in which it is worn. The same tyre spotlit in a theatre and accompanied by the sound of waves and seagulls is something else. Change the tape to the sound of a car crash and it achieves a new significance. Get one performer to stand inside it and she is given security. Get another performer to do the same and it becomes a constraint. By the introduction of performance elements the found object is suddenly given nine lives.

There's no doubt that the impetus for performance work came from such sources, taught and practised within art schools. But such notions also happened to tally with some concerns of experiments within the theatre. So the second five markers come from that area.

First: small, permanent companies rejected the role of the writer and built pieces from the particular performance abilities, interests and obsessions of individual members.

Second: freed from the text as source, theatre groups began to re-discover that a picture is worth a thousand words. Cumbersome literary devices were abandoned for the construction of eliptical, speedy and pivotal images borrowed from the techniques of film and television. Writers in turn quickly learned from these experiments in style and incorporated them within their own work.

Third: conventional theatrical structures were reconsidered together with the kind of plot developments, narratives, and approaches to character that go with them.

Fourth: forced to perform in spaces not usually equipped for theatre, companies saw the need to adapt their work to different environments. It was then a short step to the performance idea that the work should proceed from a reaction to the space in which it was to be presented.

Fifth: the work of 'multi-media' companies like Moving Being recognized the need to heal the breach between disciplines – between theatre and dance, between music and theatre, between word and image.

Such is the geography which gave rise to the peculiarly British activity of performance art. Perhaps it exists in this country only because we resolutely refuse to utilize the ability of sight as a primary means of communication in our mainstream theatre – performance work is necessarily single-minded in order to redress the imbalance. It's unlikely, though, that any of the personalities involved have sought to analyse their work in this way. And fundamentally the work is about those personalities and what they will do next.

How neat it would be to draw some useful conclusions about the direction performance art has taken over the decade, to point to a clear development of the form through experience so that we might anticipate its future. It is true that the work is often now given with greater authority, that it is better and more accurately presented, that there has been a movement towards more rigorously structured work, that new skills have been learned, that personalities and groups have deepened their interests rather than broadening them; and it is true that in this process a certain youthful exploratory vigour has been lost. But such comments are so general as to be virtually worthless. The important thing is that performance work continues to put itself at risk with every new audience and thereby remains truly experimental. When general conclusions can be reached then the work will have lost its unpredictable base and will have ossified. Fortunately there is no sign of this happening yet and younger performers are beginning to be attracted to the form as a way of life.

Of all contemporary theatre, performance art is the most ephemeral and benefits the least from any attempt at historical reconstruction. It is concerned with the living moment, with actions rather than acting, with the feeling generated at a particular gig at a particular and unrepeatable

Right: IOU in *Corners Mouth*, 1979. IOU, who broke away from Welfare State in 1976, intermesh music and visual image to make a totally non-literary narrative form. This show – for which they had half a ton of red sand delivered to the Oval House – was a non-linear epic poem set in a desertscape of an inert world. "A miner tunnels through the air held back by impassive godlike creatures, and later two blackish Magrittean figures fly a crow with one wing and walk a deathly dog. At one stage a posse of chair creatures with striped antennae and bustling tails gallop onto the stage: a joust between them is witnessed by a singing card, a demonic-looking Queen of Spades . . ." – Ann McFerran.

Hesitate and Demonstrate in *Horrid Things*, 1979. The group was formed in 1975 by Leeds arts students. Set at the seaside with enveloping yellow sand, pink crabs, funfair horse and decaying guest-house, this show precisely detailed the Gothic horrors of childhood – a world where hoovers erupted and fishes hovered. Their work is allusive, delicate and distinctively feminine in quality.

moment in time. For this reason any kind of narrative description has been avoided here. Colourful and detailed descriptions can be found elsewhere.[1]

Finally, though, it's necessary to try and give a sniff of the event, a personal view of what it was actually like to be there. Only photographic records exist as a trigger for recollection. A selection of these are offered as a more attractive alternative to a simple list of people, companies and events. Hopefully they might act as an advertisement for the work which can be seen now and next week – for the only way to understand performance art is to see it.

Reference

1 Particularly recommended are Jeff Nuttall's *Performance Art: Memoirs* (John Calder, 1979) and the quarterly magazine *Primary Sources*.

8 Product into Process
Actor-based workshops

Colin Chambers

An actor's lot is not a happy one though it has improved with the growth of publicly subsidized theatre in general and of the fringe in particular. For the fringe arose as much out of the habitual discontent of performers as out of the wider political and social changes of the sixties.

Actors are always looking for new ways of working, with more challenging parts, and this is what was created in the mushrooming of experiments that affected so many different art forms in that all too brief period of energy and expansion in Britain's postwar decline. Actors were fed up with poor contracts, insecurity, high unemployment and low pay in an industry that was a good foreign currency earner and an indispensable seedbed for other, profitable, entertainments such as television and the cinema. On top of the bad conditions of work, the roles for most actors, especially women, were frustratingly weak, small and predictable. The overall picture was still bleak despite the new regional and national subsidized theatres which, generally speaking, offered only limited opportunities to a few to break out of the traditional mould. Operating in the market economy, however 'mixed', their experiments in democracy or ensemble playing were either short-lived, half-hearted or non-existent.

The multifarious happenings of the fringe provided an escape from drawing-room comedies and spear-carrying in Shakespeare. The money, if there was any, was no better and the conditions of work were often worse but the important difference was that actors could take an equal part in the process of production. No longer disposable, cheap commodities, they could control their own work and its environment and begin to develop new relationships, first with the other participants and then with their audiences.

Actors began increasingly to cross the footlights, and to come out of the proscenium and into the halls, clubs, basements, pubs and colleges that housed these nationwide breakthroughs. Some groups performed in the streets. However temporary, inconclusive or contradictory it all was, the all-important element of democracy had been passed to actors. They gained new respect as workers in a team and were no longer seen as dilettantes, aristocrats or rabble, isolated from each other and their audiences, except for the few stars, who communicated a false image through an alienated and alienating medium.

Ironically, it was the notion and practice of the collective that allowed the individual to flower rather than the ailing market system, which claimed to be based on individual freedom while putting a few on a pedestal for a time and dumping the rest on the scrap-heap. Likewise, it was radical, egalitarian cooperation that allowed the individual actor to be more expressive and creative rather than the authoritarian relationships of the conventional theatre.

Although there was a British tradition of collective work, the main impetus in the sixties came from abroad, mainly the US, which acted as a channel for many of the mainland European experiments. Crucial events were the visits in 1967 of Cafe La Mama to the Mercury Theatre, west London, and the Open Theatre to the Royal Court. The American trend was to concentrate on a simple, trible search for myth and innocence, which preoccupied many (often middle-class) urban youths, who saw all industrial, military societies as being uncontrollably run by unknowable forces. The classic style was pioneered by the Living Theatre, which visited the Roundhouse in 1971 with its powerful, physical images of mechanized life, inspired, as many were, by the surrealist French poet, playwright and actor, Antonin Artaud.

Freehold.   The emphasis of this 'poor' theatre was on the collective re-discovery of all the senses (including the psyche), using the body rather than words as the primary means of expression. One of the most influential groups to use this approach was Freehold, which came out of Wherehouse La Mama in 1969 and stayed together until 1973. A key figure associated with Freehold was Nancy Meckler, who was one of the first people to take advantage of the Drury Lane Arts Lab when she arrived in Britain in early 1968, having worked with La Mama Plexus in New York.

Freehold was a highly disciplined ensemble which relied on the utmost physical and emotional commitment from each actor and a long time was spent in workshop before the group played publicly. The distinctive quality of their work (apart from offering strong roles for women) was the creation of non-naturalistic images through gesture and movement to present a story. The actors were not tied down to the visual or vocal demands of one 'consistent' character as in a conventional narrative. The force of *Antigone* – which re-worked Sophocles' original into an anti-war play and changed the invocations to the Gods into appeals for 'love' – was in the performance and not the hippie politics. The 'message' of *Genesis* – that we make different gods to suit ourselves – came through a physical demonstration of evolution and not a lecture on Darwinism.

Freehold's most effective work, however, grew out of a productive relationship with a writer: for example, Peter Hulton on *Antigone* and Roy

A play such as Sophocles' *Antigone* makes a powerful base from which to work. Freehold's production at the Royal Court in 1970 used strong body expression and movement to re-present the original.

Kift on *Mary Mary*. (Uniquely, *Mary Mary*, which followed the story of a girl murderer in Newcastle, showing her to be the victim of her background, was not based on a classical or mythical world, though Freehold's treatment of contemporary social reality was definitely anti-naturalistic.) The result was a balance between the physical and the verbal, overcoming British theatre's usual emphasis on the latter while avoiding some of the fringe's obsession with the former. But the tendency of the 'total' theatre groups to move toward a dramatic world no longer rooted in contemporary social reality made them less acceptable in Britain than abroad. (This affected directors like Peter Brook, for example, who left Britain to work from Paris.)

Alfredo Michelson, Shelley Lee and Steven Berkoff (right) of the London Theatre Group in Berkoff's adaptation of Edgar Allen Poe's *The Fall of the House of Usher*, at the Hampstead Theatre Club (1975).

At the other end of the spectrum were those who exploited meticulously a heightened form of naturalism through improvisation, such as Mike Leigh (*Hard Labour, Babies Grow Old, Abigail's Party*) and Mike Bradwell with Hull Truck (*Bridget's House, Bed of Roses*). Their work is always original and they release the imagination of their actors through a highly structured workshop process. Both Leigh and Bradwell usually start with an actor on his or her own, outlining the character – background, attitudes, dress, habits – in a mutual process of research, monologues, improvisations. Having worked like this with each actor separately to develop a firm idea of the character, the director brings them all together in different situations and relationships. Gradually a plot emerges as some things are thrown out and others explored. There is no script but each scene is bedded in the actors' carefully prepared development. And this – managements permitting – all takes place at its own pace and not to a rigid rehearsal deadline.

The result of this type of approach has been a distinctive 'comedy of manners', however harsh, which stresses the value of art by trying as much as possible to remove its separation from the way an audience might experience life outside the theatre. Their success depends, in the end, on the collective exploitation of the actors' personalities, expressed through their physical and mental skills under the guiding hand of an author-director. The limitation is that, since the characters are necessarily close to the actors' personal experiences, the productions tend to reflect the déclassé world of the alienated, educated youth of the late sixties.

Other groups relied entirely on the vocal and physical developments of the actors working collectively. Shared Experience, founded in 1975, focused on experimenting with story-telling, sometimes taking popular works like the *Arabian Nights* or *Bleak House* and sometimes creating their own material such as the *Science Fictions* show. This anti-naturalistic strain was kept alive in a particularly idosyncratic, not to say violent, way by Steven Berkoff.

After six years of working in rep, Steven Berkoff presented Kafka's *In the Penal Colony* at the Arts Lab in 1968. Berkoff delved into classical texts to transform them – Aeschylus, Shakespeare, Poe, Strindberg and Kafka – despite following others in the 'anti-literature as Art' boom. His London Theatre Group has performed many of his adaptations – *The Trial, Metamorphosis, Agamemnon, The Fall of the House of Usher* – as well as his own original *East*, without sets but using the actors' physical resources 'at the height of one's powers', as Berkoff puts it. Berkoff was trained in mime and is keen on non-British stylized theatre – Japanese theatre, for example. Like some latter-day actor-manager he writes, directs and acts in all the productions and his group achieves a purity of expression shaped by ritual and mime which owes a lot to his own personality and drive.

Joint Stock. Bridging the two 'extremes' of heightened naturalism and violent anti-naturalism is the Joint Stock Theatre Group which has roots in several traditions. Joint Stock, heralded by many critics as the most important experimental or fringe group of the seventies, was founded in 1974 by Max Stafford-Clark, David Hare and David Aukin, all of whom had been variously involved in fringe touring groups since the late sixties.

Stafford-Clark, Joint Stock's artistic director, had joined the Traverse Theatre in Edinburgh in 1966, three years after it had been taken over by Jim Haynes. Having seen Cafe La Mama at work, Stafford-Clark decided to try workshop productions and this led to the Traverse Theatre Workshop, which proved successful in stimulating all the participants, particularly the writer, who produced a script from the ideas put forward by the whole company.

It was this approach that he brought to Joint Stock and that freed the actors from the limitations of a three- or four-week rehearsal period tied to finished scripts that had to be learned by rote. The writer, director and designer also benefited in this way although the group did not do away with division of labour as other groups had done. However, by releasing them all within a close-knit group, the specific tasks of acting, directing, writing and designing fitted together in a new way. In the workshops the conventional relationship of god-like director manipulating puppet-like actors to a predetermined text was thrown overboard. Even during the final rehearsal period the presence of *two* directors – Stafford-Clark and William Gaskill – tended to undermine the 'norm'.

Joint Stock's first three productions were *The Speakers* (1974), *Fanshen* (1975) and *Yesterday's News* (1976) and a method of working evolved from these factually-based productions that became characteristic of the company. Several weeks are spent in workshop when the actors, directors, writer and designer work out what will become the basis of the play and script. The writer then goes away to write a text, which is then rehearsed for the production.

In *Fanshen*, which was about the experiences of one small village during the Chinese revolution, the five-week highly disciplined workshop period (the nine actors had to play some thirty different parts) allowed small groups to work on different sections of the book from which the play was adapted. This gave the group time to do research and to understand the Chinese Communists and the problems of building a new world thousands of miles away from Britain.

For *Cloud Nine* (1979), the research was into sexual politics and for *Epsom Downs* (1977) the actors went to racecourses as the play was set on Derby Day.

The workshop in action.   When the workshop began for Robert Tressell's *The Ragged-trousered Philanthropists* in 1978 there was little idea of what the result would be. The original book, often described as the first working-class novel, had deservedly been adapted several times before and another version opened in Manchester at the same time as the Joint Stock production in Plymouth. The initial problem facing the workshop was how to avoid being too historical and so failing to make the connection with modern-day conditions. Equally, there was a risk of being too concerned with making a special case about modern society and thus being dismissed as mere propaganda.

Out of this confusion came the focus and structure of the play, which turned out to be a mirror image of the workshop experience. The workshop period lasted for four weeks and was attended by seven actors, the writer Stephen Lowe, the designer Peter Hartwell and the director William Gaskill, with regular visits from other Joint Stock personnel such as the administrator who discussed the business end of the venture with everyone.[1] Before the workshop began, Lowe had formulated the question: "How does work now illustrate the problems inherent in our society?" – a question that Tressell himself had tackled. The answer came through a decisive discovery at the local Dartington College Hall, where students acted as waitresses and college staff sat at a separate table from the company – just like the bosses at the beano in the book.

Robert Tressell's ragged-trousered philanthropists in fine voice in Joint Stock's production – the result of the collaborative workshop process between actors, writer and director (1978).

The company's 'solution' led to the open-ended nature of the production, with its slow, rhythmic pace building up to the beano. For the first five minutes of the play the men unload a cart full of tools and set about their tasks in different parts of the house they are decorating (represented by flats erected in and among the audience). The men start painting, scraping and wallpapering without a word, the only audible sounds being those of their work. They start as anonymous workers performing simultaneous but isolated tasks but they finally come together as 'real' characters, gradually becoming aware of trade unionism and their group identity. This was the same process of discovery that had been made by the actors who themselves had started as 'hired hands' but emerged as people with their own personalities in an ensemble.

In the play the actors were expressing two main ideas: firstly, a celebration of the men as workers and secondly, their uneven consciousness of this. The actors had to develop a style to match the two-fold nature of the play's representation of authentic Edwardian decorators, which meant using real materials and techniques, while at the same time being distinct individuals whose thoughts could connect with a modern-day situation. They had to find the right balance between 'naturalism' and 'caricature', between the social position of the worker and his individual character.

The workshop was held mainly in a warehouse and a church hall in a working-class district of Plymouth. In the mornings the manual work was done; the warehouse had to be stripped and renovated for the Dartington students and this gave everyone the experience of using scaffolding, ladders, trestles, hammers, paintbrushes and other tools of the trade. In the afternoons and early evenings there was a mixture of games, 'choir practice' and improvisations, some 'free' and some based on scenes from the book. For example, one actor would read a scene while another mimed it, or the actors would dress in bizarre, second-hand costumes and have to hold their character without speaking while images and situations changed. Another technique was to play a scene naturalistically and in rather a throwaway manner but at the same time stressing any inner thoughts or asides in a heavily stylized way.

At one point, when the author felt that the actors were not sympathizing with the characters as human beings but as specimens under a microscope, each actor went out and talked to someone in the building and decorating trade. He then returned to the group to play that person and to be questioned by the others about him and then to repeat the process as a character from the book. At times there was the problem of being too 'real' and too much themselves, forgetting, for example, the deference that was characteristic of workers in the Edwardian age. They had to use their own personalities to register both an historical and a modern truth, the one through the other.

Improvisations were carried out to show how capitalism lowers working standards and makes 'time equal money', or how status sticks outside of its original environment. Underlying all the work was the need for the actors to find out how character is not fixed or eternal but is shaped by social relationships. This was helped by changing parts all the time as well as the exercises. In the production everyone played two or three roles. Five of the seven actors, including the one woman, played the foreman Hunter, whose jacket and bowler hat were ritually placed at the end of each turn on a dummy in the centre of the acting area. A foreman is a foreman is a foreman. . . and two of the 'class enemy' were represented by dummies in one scene.

All in all the workshop was successful, particularly as it was held out of London, since this led to better social contact after the long hours of work than is usually the case in the capital. It had started with Gaskill being strict about routine and acting styles, emphasizing and showing the importance of props, which is often neglected in other traditions. As the workshop progressed the actors came to know each other and to take more decisions for themselves while Gaskill acted as an authoritative guide, though still very much the director. The actors worked on their own for two days and gradually took more of a part in organizing the work schedule, deciding which scenes or parts they would tackle, discussing the shape of the play, criticizing their own work as well as that of others, and dealing with the business aspects of the production. A tribute to their achievement was that, after the eight-week gap during which Lowe wrote his script, the group came back together for its six weeks of rehearsal and clicked straight away. With late casting and a lot of rewriting, the company produced one of the outstanding shows of the seventies.

Joint Stock managed to achieve a remarkable consistency in its approach to acting – spare and unrhetorical in style but precise and flexible. It developed an extraordinary ability to define, fix and hold character whether the actor was playing the smallest or the largest part, or both. It could cope with hilarious cartoon, as in Barrie Keeffe's Silver Jubilee spoof *A Mad World, My Masters* or with the tough, television-type naturalism of *Yesterday's News*. The approach was suited to closer contact with the audience than most West End or regional proscenium theatres allowed. In *The Speakers*, even more than in the Tressell, the action took place among the audience and often simultaneously. Performances have therefore tended to be for 'arena' or three-sided venues. However, when Gaskill took some of the company to the National's open 1,160-seat Olivier auditorium to do *A Fair Quarrel* the low-key style was swallowed up and the production vanished. On the other hand, in *Epsom Downs* the nine actors, who played 43 parts (including horses) on a specially designed green slope, easily filled the 850-seat Roundhouse.

The strength of the company, apart from building a regular following around Britain as it tours, can be seen in its influence on other theatres, and other media, whether it is the reps, the RSC, the National, or the Royal Court, for which it has provided a source of high-level acting as well as a string of excellent productions. This exchange has been characteristic of the fringe as a whole, where many groups have used the same workshop method, if in a slightly modified form. It differs from the American practice of actors losing themselves in a primeval scream because it emphasizes the role each has to play and builds character on that understanding – an understanding not necessarily inherent in the text. The change in working conditions from the conventional was designed to produce more effective theatre and not as personal therapy (though that may have happened as a bonus).

The general shift in attitudes from the 'product' to the 'process', brought about in part by the fringe, was democratic and, as a source of new ideas and values, reached well beyond the generation of young radicals. Battles were won to get both the Arts Council and Equity to recognize the fringe, though training has not been affected as much as it should have been. Responding to a growing desire by actors to control their destinies, highly regarded actors such as Ian McKellen and Edward Petherbridge formed the Actors Company in 1972 to achieve a good standard of acting across the board in more traditional productions by equally strong casting through-out. Though teamwork was not new to the British theatre – it lay behind Brook's best work – it was generally not democratic and often led to the creation of new stars (e.g. Alan Howard), which made ensemble playing impossible. Mechanical application of democracy does not work either: for example, the RSC's 1970 season at Stratford-upon-Avon in which leading actors awkwardly played walk-ons (though not all walk-ons played leads). Yet the fringe did help to influence the RSC when it developed its small-scale work through The Other Place and The Ware-house, which offered a more challenging mix to an actor of classical and modern plays.

Peter Hall at the National wanted to solve his problems by setting up a separate company for each auditorium but only the Cottesloe has achieved anything approaching this. While hardly presenting experimental work as was first promised, a core of actors under director Bill Bryden, and often with writer Keith Dewhurst, has developed a style through mainly folksy 'promenade' productions that take a cosy look at England's history, apparently offering what the fringe does but without the edge. However, their popularity and moments of success (as in *The World Turned Upside Down*) show the strength of the principle.

The fringe also raised other issues, for example the lack of good parts for women. Monstrous Regiment was set up in 1976 on the basis of always having more women than men in the company and to tackle related problems, such as sexism on the rehearsal floor or child care provision. Many fringe groups stayed as workshop-based cooperatives throughout the seventies but had to face the practical difficulties of meeting the Arts Council's grant requirements, of ensuring the group's own continuity, and dealing with the problem of the ultimate power of a non-acting figure – usually the director. Joint Stock had started out as a management with a board that hired actors for a show. It overcame the authoritarian division of labour problem through the relative luxury of long workshop and rehearsal periods, in which *all* roles were allowed to be more fully expressed rather than just that of the director. With the formation of a permanent company in 1977 the actors demanded full say in its running and not just in the production process. But when that company left and a new one emerged, the collective idea had to be rethought. The result is a two-tier set-up. First there is the group working on the current production, which controls all the affairs of that particular production; second there is a larger policy committee that takes care of longer-term questions. This second group includes the first group.

Although the mixed economy briefly allowed the expansion of different trends in alternative theatre, from the 'physical' to the 'social', market pressures are always around the corner. The appeal of the West End for actors may not be as strong as it once was but the lure of television and, more recently, of the national companies, dominates their working lives. These pressures effectively prevent the formation of permanent acting companies. Yet actors will only gain a true measure of democratic control over their own work within such a structure. For the moment the set-up of Joint Stock and many other groups is only a compromise. Nevertheless the fact that alternative theatre has been able to change the organization of the production process, and that its experiments in cooperative democracy have had so many imitators in the more hierarchical world of the state-subsidized rep theatre system with its twin pinnacles of the Royal Shakespeare Company and the National Theatre, is some measure of its success. How permanent the changes in working method are will be tested in the next few years under a Conservative government seemingly un-attached to the idea of state subsidy of the arts and in an overall cultural climate where the definition of experiment gets more conservative every day.

Reference

1 This account is based upon *Joint Stock and The Ragged-trousered Philanthropists: Letters from a Workshop* by Stephen Lowe, Dartington Theatre Papers No. 2, Series III; plus discussions with Joint Stock personnel.

9 Voicing the Protest

The new writers

Steve Grant

The British theatre in the twentieth century has been a history of its dramatists, and though the traditional demarcation lines have been somewhat erased by the activity of the fringe, the theatre as a whole continues to depend for much of its effectiveness on the achievements of playwrights.

In 1979 the *British Alternative Theatre Directory* listed over 120 writers working in professional theatre while the playwright's union, the Theatre Writers' Union (TWU), boasted over 150 members. However, it can be argued that those writers who have really shaped the concerns of contemporary theatre since 1968 number less than ten. Their work adds up to a solid body of social and political comment, formal invention and verbal eloquence which, although indebted to the previous generation of playwrights, differs significantly in at least three vital respects. Firstly, the abolition of stage censorship in 1968 allowed greater licence of language and imagination than had been possible before. (Perhaps because the habits of writing under censorship had become too deeply engrained, older writers have been unable to enjoy this new-found freedom – though some have attempted to exploit it.) Secondly, the new playwrights, most of whom were born in the late nineteen-forties, were positively fired by the political and cultural upheavals of the period whereas the previous generation tended to suffer from an unfocused social disenchantment. Thirdly, they were convinced that their work could only have meaning or effect through a search for new audiences in new venues.

As time has passed the division between the fringe and mainstream theatre has become eroded. Partly this can be explained by the traditional progression of the 'better' playwrights from fringe or avant-garde to the mainstream, from cult status to wider acceptance. Portable Theatre is a case in point. Founded in 1968 by two Cambridge undergraduates, Tony Bicat and David Hare, who were convinced that if the old theatre audiences didn't want their wares then new ones composed of their peers could be found who did, Portable Theatre was a seminal and profoundly Anglo-Saxon force. It promoted three of our most distinctive writers:

Howard Brenton, David Hare and Snoo Wilson. By 1973, however, these writers were convinced that the time had come to break into the established theatre (and onto the larger stages). Portable Theatre was disbanded. By the end of the seventies all three writers were writing almost exclusively for the established subsidized theatre. It is difficult to say whether Portable's audiences have followed it into the established theatre. Perhaps anyway the idealistic student generation of the late sixties has itself mellowed into the middle-class comfort of early middle age. Nevertheless, all three writers (and the others considered in this chapter) still remain distinctively different from the older writers with whom they now share the stage.

However, a view of the theatre today tends to notice the similarities across the board. Ten years ago it was the differences which were picked out. In fact, playwrights have always crossed the boundary between fringe and established theatre. Thus, in the early seventies Trevor Griffiths was writing for both the Royal Shakespeare Company and 7:84; David Hare with Portable Theatre and the Hampstead Theatre Club; and Howard Barker started out in the Royal Court. Except for playwrights like John McGrath, who works exclusively with the company he formed (7:84), most writers are freelance producers working on their own outside the companies. Thanks to the greatly increased funds to writers made possible by the Arts Council's New Writing Sub-Committee of the Drama Panel, writers now tend to be commissioned by companies before writing their plays, rather than writing them on spec. The common image of the writer as an isolated figure perfecting his masterpiece alone in a garret is no longer true − if it ever was. Writers are now much more closely involved in the production process, attending rehearsals and so on, while companies have more prior say in the subject matter of the play. This is a welcome step towards more cooperative relations of production but essentially the writer's freelance position remains unaltered.

Alternative theatre companies can be considered historically and critically within the context of the movement of which they are part. Writers, on the other hand, though the ones considered here share much of the ideology of the companies, must be studied individually and through an examination of their plays precisely because of their position of limited independence within the process of making theatre.

Howard Brenton and David Hare: *From Portable to Permanence*

"I do believe that people do go clinically mad if what they believe bears no relation to how they live . . ." David Hare, 1975[1]

"I think the theatre's a real bear pit. It's not the place for reasoned discussion. It is the place for really savage insights, which can be proved at once . . ." Howard Brenton, 1975[2]

A critic once hesitatingly dubbed Brenton and Hare the Lennon and McCartney of the New Wave.[3] Indeed, the comparison has its point. Brenton is most at home when creating startling and often outrageous *coups de théâtre* or when composing choice, vernacular exchanges for his favourite characters, who are usually villains, policemen or angry, disenfranchised youngsters.

Hare once confessed, albeit wryly, that he can only write about the middle classes;[4] and while it is true that he can pen convincing dialogue for Chinese peasants or zonked-out rock musicians, his most memorable creations stem from the highly articulate but often emotionally sterile bourgeoisie. Hare is particularly concerned with the sufferings of intense and virulently honest people (often women) caught up in the cloying, claustrophobic and tightly knit society of establishment Britain, whether it be the suburban delights of stockbroker Guildford, the groves of academe or the post-Suez diplomatic service.

In Hare's plays the rules of the game are often the only important factors. Those who survive are those who *know* the rules. In Brenton's best plays the struggle is between the will to violent, often destructive action and the need for slow and careful political consciousness-raising. Brenton's plays pose the problem of the possibility of revolutionary change in a country whose traditions are draped like a blanket over everything that threatens its security. Hare's plays depict that society, often from the inside and at its most dangerously attractive.

Not surprisingly Hare has shifted somewhat in his attitude to his own work. When *Plenty* opened at the National Theatre in 1977 he said: "A play is a performance. So if a play is to be a weapon in the class struggle, then the weapon is not going to be the things you are saying: it is the interaction of what you are saying and what the audience is thinking. The play is in the air."[5] This statement seems to indicate a rejection of overt political preaching.

Brenton has fewer fears about the content of his plays, seeing himself in the epic theatrical tradition of Brecht, a playwright politicized by his own writings. Even in his most accessible play to date – *Epsom Downs* – Brenton creates a vivid dramatic tension out of his various characters, all imprisoned within the gloriously absurd confines of the Big Occasion and yet all faced with the possibility of change. For Emily Davison, the suffragette who threw herself beneath the King's horse at the Epsom Derby in 1913, change means violent self-sacrifice; for a young homeless couple who have blown their savings on Lester Piggott and the Minstrel, change is realizing that winning the money for a home doesn't finally mean anything; for Jocks, the sacked stable lad, change means an articulation of his embryonic class awareness; for Tillotson, the evangelist, change means rejecting the hypodermic of religion for the bigger if equally illusory thrill of the wager. And in the most telling speech in the play, Margaret, the

Joint Stock actors Tony Rohr and
Will Knightley as horse and rider on
Derby Day in *Epsom Downs* by
Howard Brenton.

homeless housewife, muses while queuing for the ladies:

> "I hate the fat happy people on the grass with their teeth stuck in
> chicken drums, Jubilee flags coming out of their hairy ears. Minds red
> with booze and bets. If I get a pee will I have to join in? Have a good
> time again? Love my husband and children again? Not feel choked by
> the gas of a good time had by all."[6]

This expression of inner disenchantment mixed with a muted desire to
belong is quite typical of the power and ambiguity of the best of Brenton's
work. Indeed, what is not always appreciated by critics of both Brenton
and Hare is the conflicts which arise within their plays – conflicts that are
not necessarily (though at times they certainly can be) the result of
confusion on the part of the dramatist but merely reflections of the

complexity of their creations. One critic went so far as to dub the entire generation represented by these two authors as *The Wild Bunch*,[7] and others have often approached the plays in question from the point of view of discrediting their 'Marxist' intentions. If the plays are full of contradictions and doubts then that is not necessarily a fault. Both Hare and Brenton are deeply concerned with morality, with the need for compassion and courage, and with the fears and desperations of their contemporaries. It is these features as much as any strident cry for revolutionary change that permeate their work.

Magnificence (1973), Brenton's examination of urban terrorism – a theme he has returned to in *The Saliva Milkshake* (1975) and *Weapons of Happiness* (1976) – exhibits a classic ambiguity. Jed the bomber blows himself up in the bungled course of assassinating a Tory Minister. While the audience strongly identifies with Jed, who has been politicized through his experiences in a brutal squat eviction, it is his companion Cliff who pronounces the supposedly telling verdict. For Jed the act of extreme destructiveness is "magnificent", for Cliff it is "a fucking stupid gesture" which has reduced Jed to "a nothing. A zero. A crank with a tin box of bangs." But with which verdict does the audience identify? Theatrically with Jed, politically (Brenton obviously hopes) with Cliff for whom action is "work, corny work, with and for the people".

Weapons of Happiness and *The Churchill Play* represent Brenton's work at its most expansive. *The Churchill Play*, set in an internment camp in 1984 after a coalition government takeover backed by the military, is a nightmare vision of the future in which Churchill, the pinnacle of National Heroism, is portrayed through a play-within-a-play as a hypochondriac and obsessive, out of touch with the British people and haunted by a spectre of gloom called Black Dog. At the climax of the play various internees attempt to escape and are glimpsed finally in the glare of the camp searchlights. Earlier another prisoner has called off the attempt, preferring to stay alive, to survive ". . . in the cracks. Either side of the wire."

In *Weapons of Happiness*, which was written for the newly opened National Theatre's Lyttleton auditorium, Brenton has extended his field of vision to take in the bitter example of the Stalinist betrayal in Eastern Europe. The play, impressive in its technical virtuosity, juxtaposes the sufferings of a former Czech Communist leader, Joseph Frank, imprisoned, tortured and tried in the 1952 Slansky show trials (and in reality hanged) with the fumblings and sometimes ludicrous gropings towards political awareness of a group of South London factory workers. There is a perennial problem in the play, namely that the representatives of the contemporary capitalist classes are poor creations indeed, as if Brenton's invention had run out before reaching them. Thus the factory owner (typically it's a potato crisp factory, which makes for much humour but detracts from the play's seriousness) writes poetry and reacts to the occupation of his works by drinking champagne, dissecting his marriage with an equally unbelievable rich-bitch wife ("I would like you all to know back there that he never liked me to touch my breasts") and consuming himself in vitriolic worker-bashing. As Charles Marowitz observed the picture is not only uncritical but positively inaccurate.[8]

It seems that on occasion Brenton's love of comedy and violent theatrical confrontation robs him of a much-needed analytical element. There is simply very little contest in the play between the capitalist classes and their real or potential opponents, even though the latter comprise a portentous Czech, a deaf mute, an illiterate, an old lag and a few sullen, inarticulate boys and girls. Nevertheless *Weapons of Happiness* contains much that is good about Brenton's work. It has a dimension that so much political theatre lacks (and not merely because it could utilize the National Theatre's gallery of computerized stage effects), ranging as it does from the New Testament of Christ to the Cosmos of the Planetarium, from the winter streets of post-war Moscow to the rural landscape of contemporary Wales. At its climax the factory employees start afresh (leaving Frank dead of a heart attack), bent on a slow process of self-help. It is certainly a bleak and tentative conclusion, not without hope but almost a thin, bare gesture when set against the ferocity of Frank's torment. Indeed, there are three texts for the play: Hicks, the Labour Party union organizer (another stereotype of the period) – "See, the best you can hope for in this world is to nudge! Give it a bit of a nudge." Alf, the surly worker: "If I kick in the telly and pour Harpic over the window box, will things get any better? On the whole I'd say . . . Yes." And Frank: "Nothing will change in England. Decay, yes. Change, no." It is the great achievement of Brenton's play that these three assertions are almost simultaneously displayed. Yet the final word is left with the audience.

Brenton's earlier work is notable for its theatrical invention, particularly the intriguing use of environmental elements. Early plays include a portrait of *Wesley*, performed in a suitably denominational church, a version of Rabelais' *Gargantua*, with the pioneering fringe company Brighton Combination, played out in the representation of a giant stomach, and *Scott of the Antarctic*, performed in 1971 on a Bradford ice rink with one professional actor, several amateurs, skaters, a rock band and a performance artist. His first major success, *Christie in Love* (1969), takes a new look at the notorious mass murderer as a clue to society's own sexual hypocrisies. It is most notable for its brilliantly evocative design (a play-pen made out of newspaper) and its effective juxtaposition of various dramatic styles – from the baldly naturalistic to the comically grotesque. Brenton's first full-length play, *Revenge* (1969), though small beer in comparison with later works, has a pleasing comic intensity (as much gleaned from the radio humour of the time as from prior theatrical models) and as well as dramatizing the voice of Brixton Gaol – "Oh England, what will become of you . . .?" – has both main parts played by the same actor: the old criminal Adam Hepple and his arch-rival, a religious detective inspector named Macleish.

In many of Brenton's earlier plays the obsessional qualities of his central protagonists play a major role in the moral content. In the words of Peter Ansorge: "Brenton's protagonists are frustrated not by the judgements of their society – but the lack of any definite moral code of justice."[9] Though there are great weaknesses of judgement in some of these early dramatic excursions (what is the author's view on Christie, for example, other than as a barometer of officially sanctioned passions?) the emphasis on the need for individual integrity, the search for codes which transcend the pragmatic or the habitual, is well to the fore. It is also a preoccupation of Brenton's long-time friend and sometime director and collaborator, David Hare.

David Hare, born in 1948, the son of a merchant seaman (officer class) is commonly regarded as the most blatantly talented theatrical worker of his generation – and also the most difficult to classify. A superbly gifted director of both his own plays and those of his contemporaries, Hare was a co-founder both of Portable Theatre in 1968 and of Joint Stock some six years later. He came relatively late to play-writing, claiming to have despised dramatists for their uselessness and self-pity. Indeed, only when a Portable-commissioned play failed to turn up did he start, with the comedy *How Brophy Made Good*.

Hare's contribution to contemporary drama begins in earnest in 1974 with *Knuckle*, written for the progressive West End producer Michael Codron. It is followed by *Fanshen*, an adaptation of William Hinton's book about a Chinese village in the aftermath of revolution, *Teeth 'N' Smiles* (1975) and *Plenty*, the theatre companion to his widely acclaimed television film, *Licking Hitler*, staged at the Lyttleton in 1977. Two early plays, *Slag* (1970) and *The Great Exhibition* (1972) are pieces of more than passing interest. The first is a Genet-style sexual comedy in which three women, seemingly ensconced within a girl's public school, make merry with various burning issues of the day, women's rights and revolutionary feminism prominently among them. Hare is very much the university wit of his generation, despite having left Cambridge before completing his degree, and *Slag* is typical of his tendency to send up the progressive sections of society as much as their reactionary counterparts. Also typical are the literary or formal elements in the writing; on one level *Slag* is a parody of the opening scene of *Love's Labour's Lost. The Great Exhibition*, Hare admits quite unrepentently, came out of his experience as literary manager of the Royal Court between 1969–70 and can be seen as a technically accomplished send-up of the archetypal Royal Court play: working-class Labour MP, disillusioned with public and private life, takes to flashing on Clapham Common while employing a private dick to trail his middle-class spouse.

Hare's preoccupation with the corrupting effect of capitalism forms the basis of *Knuckle*, another formally inventive comedy thriller that transposes the affluent, secretive world of a Raymond Chandler novel into the smarter echelons of Surrey society. Like so many of Hare's plays *Knuckle* opens in an atmosphere of teasing obscurity: a bar, a dance band. Are we in LA? No, it's Guildford, and why is the laconic young man drinking lemonade? Curly Delafield is an international arms dealer who returns home to investigate the disappearance of his sister Sarah. In the course of his investigations Curly exposes the monied values of his father's society and falls for a friend of Sarah's, Jenny, only to lose her finally.

Knuckle is a fascinating piece of writing, on one level an affectionate parody of the clipped style of the labyrinthine thriller, and indeed of the drama of parental discord (Curly's stockbroker father barely acknowledges the existence of his children while being engrossed in the novels of Henry James), on another a biting comment on the damaging effect of acquisitive life-styles on potentially worthwhile lives. Indeed, Curly's refusal to act on his knowledge comes as little surprise, given his rather bizarre defence of his own occupation – both as a reaction to his father's more respectable exploitation and as a service to world peace! And though Hare's satirical inclinations sometimes overbalance, there is a newly found compassion and concern in *Knuckle* that marks a new departure for its author.

The survivor in Curly's glimpsed world filled "with the soft pulping of money" is his father, Patrick, whose paternal advice includes: "You've never grown up until you appreciate the value of tact. It's not a question of talent. It's a question of noise."

The statement is echoed and re-echoed in both *Teeth 'N' Smiles* and *Plenty*. *Teeth 'N' Smiles*, a hit at the Royal Court in 1975 where it was produced to coincide with the new directorial regime of Nicholas Wright and Robert Kidd, is Hare's only autobiographical play to date and it depicts one zany, self-destructive night in the life of a rock band on the blink, whose terminal gig takes them to a Cambridge May Ball in 1969. Maggie, the lead singer, is perpetually caught between bouts of drunken catatonia and egocentric nihilism. The members of the band, when not engaged in crushingly boring, time-consuming games, are busy establishing their hatred of the student audience. The bass player, Peyote, is a stumbling pharmacy and, as the audience is informed with the aid of a concluding series of slides, the only real victim: dying of a drug-related inhalation of vomit some four years later. The representatives of the dreaded university consist of a put-upon porter, Snead, who reappears at the close of the first act to instigate a bust, and a medical student, Anson, a safe figure of fun whose attempt to interview Maggie for the student rag leads him to a bout of sex behind the cricket pavilion and eventual incarceration in hospital recovering from the effects of LSD.

The play is a fascinating piece, concerned as it is with youthful idealism and its wastefulness and self-delusion. Arthur, the pivotal figure, an ex-Cambridge student who dropped out to write songs and who is still madly in love with Maggie, represents the kind of moral earnestness which on a more academic level typifies the very university he has come to hate: the Leavisite belief in significance and intelligence coupled with the need for intellectual distancing. Arthur's rebellion is a front, an aesthetic illusion reinforced by his unhappy love affair with Maggie. Maggie's own gesture of taking the rap for the bust without complaint is itself equally futile, a self-defeating burst of nervous anarchic energy ("somebody's got to keep on the move"), little different in acid-dream essence from the more gross excesses of her musicians. The play fails to take into account the more impressive achievements of Cambridge intellectualism but in doing so it does not underestimate the power of the system that Cambridge is made to symbolize. The band may have insulted a few rich punters, stolen a few trinkets, and set fire to the champagne tent but the place remains barely touched. The most cynically durable element in the proceedings is the group's manager, Saraffian, whose survival instinct was forged from his experiences during the London blitz on the Cafe de Paris. Saraffian tells how he felt someone looting his body and how, after staggering out, he saw a cabby refusing to ferry the wounded to hospital because he didn't want blood all over his "fucking taxi". Saraffian tells the story as an example of the class war which he says is always going on – "a war of attrition". This set piece is stunningly powerful but in typical Hare fashion is followed by an equally stinging counter-attack from Maggie.

As a piece of social history *Teeth 'N' Smiles* is prone to a certain subjectivity. Hare's picture of violent confrontation between working-class rock musicians and upper-class student twits seems particularly inaccurate. There was in fact far more mutual flattery between the two groups and far more collaborative good will. And while 1969 may seem a good time in which to set such a mournful play, coming as it does after the frustrated optimism of the previous year, the resulting thesis is a little too pat. Historical movements take a little time to permeate through the community. It could be argued that the kind of revolutionary, drug-orientated optimism of the '68 period did not escape the university campuses until much later. Nevertheless *Teeth 'N' Smiles* remains a fine achievement, not least because it was written for Hare's own generation and because it so mercilessly exposes the very weaknesses which others may, in moments of intellectual turpitude or easy idealism, mistake for strengths.

Hare's most recent notable stage play, *Plenty*, is in many ways his most ambitious to date and certainly his most solidly heroic. In Hare's own

David Hare's *Plenty*, with Me Me Lai, Kate Nelligan (centre) and Julie Covington.

words, *Plenty* is inspired by the ". . . belief that people died literally in vain. That the upsurge of radical feeling in the war and post-war years was a genuine outcome of their experiences and not an accident, that the emotional and material plenty of that last period of affluence was wasted, and that the British have drawn a mantle of lies and coldness over the war."[10]

In *Knuckle* Curly talks of there being "no excuses left", and such a feeling cuts right through *Plenty*, which depicts in a series of scenes which move backwards and forwards between 1943 and 1962 the experiences of its heroine, Susan. She is intelligent, arrogant, undervalued and eventually almost completely mad. Her problem is her inability to cope with the mediocrity, deception and compromise forced on her by her post-war experiences in affluent, stultifying Britain. During the war, as a young SOAS courier she had experienced the tenderness, comradeship and courage which she finally attempts to recapture some twenty years later in a brief Blackpool reunion with a young officer she last met in wartime France. In between she has drifted aimlessly through jobs in advertising, and the civil service, has attempted unsuccessfully to have a child by a working-class acquaintance, and finally marries a lack-lustre diplomat, Brock, abandoning him at the close of the play and giving their Knightsbridge home to a Battered Mothers organization run by an old bohemian friend.

As a vehicle for the actress Kate Nelligan (also seen in *Knuckle*) *Plenty* proved very successful but there was widespread and well-founded scepticism about Hare's attempt to relate Susan's own deeply felt and frenzied experiences to the wider context of post-war Britain. This was most successful in its relation to the decline of ethical standards in Brock's own field, in which his first boss, Darwin, is shown failing to recover from the treachery of Suez while his later boss, Charleson, is only concerned with the rules: "Behaviour is all" he intones when Susan threatens suicide in an attempt to save Brock's crumbling diplomatic career. Even more problematic is the overall attitude to Susan herself, whose often maddening and elitist posturings destroy any prior sympathy for her one-woman protest movement. She shoots at the failed father of her unborn child and when Brock calls her "selfish, brutish, unkind" in a blazing stand-up row the comment seems truer than the author would obviously care to believe. Nevertheless *Plenty* is an impressive work, splendidly witty and meticulous in its reconstruction of educated, diplomatic conversation. Of the female characters only Susan comes close to being a rounded creation but, in this creation of Susan, Hare has written his most colossal role to date. Judged as a yardstick for human behaviour her brand of rebellion has met with some daunting attacks from Hare's erstwhile fellow travellers in the more austere corridors of the fringe, and he remains a suspicious and often uneasy figure in such circles. However, his intelligence, despite its tendency towards show-off cleverness, and his moral sense, despite its occasional degeneration into a superior moralizing tone, make him an intriguing and important talent.

No consideration of Hare and Brenton, however brief, would be complete without a mention of *Brassneck*, their 1974 collaboration to mark the appointment of Richard Eyre as Artistic Director of the Nottingham Playhouse. *Brassneck*, a project described by the writers as "indivisible"[11] is a big play, written for a cast of twenty and containing nearly thirty characters. (Sadly it has not been seen in London though it has been televized.) It spans the years between 1945 and 1973, covering the history of three grafting generations of a Midlands commercial dynasty. Alfred Bagley is a seemingly decrepit septuagenarian who through much wheeling and dealing comes to control the property end of a small Midlands town to which he had hitch-hiked on VE day; his nephew Roderick is a Poulson-style architect whose all-party empire finally crashes through bad management and shoddy workmanship; Sidney, Roderick's sadistic, spivvy son, closes the play with a toast "to the last days of capitalism" after launching the clan on its latest business venture – heroin trafficking.

Brassneck is crammed with the virtues and predilections of its two authors: Hare's verbal wit and love of sarcastic deflation, his grasp of the rules of power, and Brenton's theatrical gusto and acute political curiosity. And though the play can be seen as a fierce attack on the acquisitive society and in particular the "masonic gangs who carved up post-war England" (Hare)[12] it betrays an almost Jonsonian delight in villainy and exudes a lack of sentiment that is almost ferocious. In *Brassneck*, though Brenton and Hare are never of the devil's party, they seem more at home with the deceptions of old Bagley and the recriminations of his awful successors than with the muted voices of protest and apology. The play is a marvellous piece of theatre which, though undoubtedly inspired by the revelations of corruption in the early 1970s, far outruns its immediate social context. One can only hope that its stage history is not already at an end.

Snoo Wilson: *Through the Distorting Mirror*

> "The good thing about the theatre is that it's always there. The bad thing is that it's gone so quickly." Snoo Wilson, 1979[13]

Snoo Wilson is the youngest of the Portable Theatre trio discussed in this chapter and he seems the least likely to be assimilated into the theatrical mainstream. Indeed, while Hare and Brenton use devices that upset the unities of time and place or deliberately distance the audience, both are comparatively conventional playwrights. Wilson, on the other hand, has a more anarchic imagination; this not only manifests itself in his subject matter (which often deals with the oppressive effect of social systems on the individual psyche) but in his formal invention and originality.

For Wilson the theatre is the freest medium, an empty space in which there should be few rules and many possibilities. Since his early career with Portable (as director and actor as well as writer) Wilson has remained true to his particular artistic beliefs. As a result his plays are not always

"Lead paint, ecology and Irish republicanism." Snoo Wilson's typically ambiguous short play *A Greenish Man* at the Bush Theatre (1978).

understood or liked by critics or by managements. (Both *The Glad Hand* and *Flaming Bodies* were successes after having been turned down by the commissioning theatre/company.) Nevertheless Wilson's plays usually do get produced somewhere (often on the fringe) while his reputation has increasingly taken on the dimensions of a minor cult.

In a Wilson play gorillas or a swan may enter during conversation, a car may crash through a plate glass window, or an act of resurrection may be accomplished on a bar room floor. Verbal communication, as one critic noted, is continually being interrupted by other forms.[14] But when the occasion demands it he can pen passages of compelling eloquence that are even more effective because of their stylistic contrast with what has gone before – rather in the way that Shakespeare uses theatrical metaphors to heighten the 'reality' of the action. Thus in *The Glad Hand* (1978), a labyrinthine fantasy set on a ship bound for the Bermuda Triangle, we are presented with an authentic description of a cowboy strike of the 1880s. In *A Greenish Man* (1978), a zany banquet is marked by a chilling monologue on the current situation in Northern Ireland. While Wilson's plays are noted for, and occasionally hampered by, their flagrant flaunting of dramatic conventions, at their most effective they contain an associative logic which can tie in and tie up such seemingly disparate topics as the Old Testament and LA Feminism, the collective paranoia of apartheid society and offbeat anthropology, and lead paint, ecology and Irish republicanism.

By the time he was 26 Wilson had already produced an impressive and original body of work: *Pignight, Blowjob, Vampire, The Beast* and *The Pleasure Principle*. All of these plays are stamped with Wilson's stylistic cleverness and with many of his recurring themes: world pollution, moral anarchy, physical decay, the occult, and the life-denying consequences of all rigid systems of ethical behaviour. Wilson is a free-wheeling writer and his own brand of erudition and reliance on layers of experience which outrun the rational and the everyday, mark him out as a vital and fertile contributor to the often mundane and socially preoccupied modern theatre landscape. And of all the playwrights discussed here, Wilson is the one most at home with the dream-like landscapes of performance arts groups such as Lumiere and Son and The People Show. At its worst his work falls foul of the 'freedom without responsibility' which can characterize such theatre. In abandoning conventional rules Wilson sometimes fails to provide alternatives. If one has problems with detail or even with a character's exit line it can be a too easy solution to wave a magic wand of anti-naturalistic abandonment over the entire proceedings. More pertinently, Wilson's kind of theatre is made up of slapstick comedy, bizarre gimmickry and a good deal of precise, intellectually coherent thought. Occasionally the tension between these seemingly contrasting impulses fails to be resolved; the result can be obscurity, self-indulgence and even boredom. Wilson is certainly a less consistent playwright than Hare or Brenton but at his best he can be devastatingly good.

If *Soul of the White Ant* had not been conceived for lunchtime performance at the small Soho Poly theatre its initial impact would probably have been greater. (A certain snobbery about play length still exists and only Samuel Beckett seems to be safe from its clutches.) The play, written in 1975, is one of Wilson's best, complete, and far from improved when it was lengthened for evening performance at the Bush Theatre after its initial run. The title derives from one of Eugene Marais' pseudo-scientific anthropological works. Marais, who died in 1936 of morphine addiction, is a classic Wilson figure. Like Crowley of *The Beast*, he is a charlatan and a visionary, both outcast and cult figure. He both embodies and defies the South African society from which he came, and in his theories about the corporate soul Wilson has found a compelling theatrical metaphor for the claustrophobic, finely balanced, closed society of apartheid. The play's ostensible setting is a grotty, mud-caked bar run by a boozy eccentric called Mabel. Her friends and customers are a red-necked journalist and two rather repressed women, Edith and June. Cutting through this rather pathetic small-town society is the threat of madness and holocaust, an ever-present danger in many of Wilson's plays (particularly in *Blowjob* and *Pignight* with their schizoids and porcine cannibals) brought by the arrival of Marais, first as a mud-caked figure of prophecy and finally as a white-suited smoothy who ostentatiously fixes with morphine at the bar. Wilson's introduction of Marais is typical: a monster risen from the ant-heap, he reveals his vision to the lager-swilling sport-obsessed journalist, de Groot, who remains unaffected. Marais' initial 'visitation' has devastating consequences. Mabel, the Ant Mother, goes batty and shoots her houseboy, whose carefully collected sperm is now filling her freezer. When the stuff is thrown into the river it impregnates June and Edith who have been bathing there. It is Marais, returned as a back-street abortionst, who rescues them: a miracle worker preserving the integrity of the community but at the cost of Mabel's bizarre act of racial violence and genetic perversity. *Soul of the White Ant* is one of the best short plays written since 1968. Wilson's gift for comic ingenuity and the selective process by which seemingly diverse images and ideas are worked into a decidedly harmonious whole is fully realized. (Some credit should also go to director Dusty Hughes, who guided both versions and whose touch was impeccable.)

Wilson's most ambitious play to date is undoubtedly *The Glad Hand* which after a long delay was finally seen at the Royal Court in 1978 in a brilliantly inventive production by Max Stafford-Clark. It is certainly no justice to the complexity and vitality of the piece even to attempt a description of the plot, which centres upon the efforts of a South African fascist called Ritsaat to locate and confront the Anti-Christ. Ritsaat's method is typically Wilsonian. He charters an oil tanker, humourlessly offers 'cowboy fun' and with a crew that includes a family of stage Paddy Irish, two camp actors, a portly American scriptwriter, a Cuban cook, a CIA agent and a dubious psychic surgeon, Ritsaat heads for the Bermuda Triangle hoping to set up a time warp and to travel back in time to the Wyoming cowboy strike of 1886 – one of the more recent sightings of the Communist devil whose destruction Ritsaat seeks.

The Glad Hand works on many levels: the cowboy strike is created on board ship as a play within a play; a raunchy American lesbian arrives on board, triggering off many of the play's spiralling coincidences; on a level approaching the political the final alliance of Irish chauvinist and Cuban cook to kill Ritsaat points to the revolutionary potential which Wilson sees embodied in the historical process, which, he implies, has shape however strange it may appear to be, and which still presents the possibility of change and progress. As Ritsaat exclaims just before his death: "The world exists as it is because people believe it to be so . . . I'm not fooled. Between you and your perceptions is the mirror which you think reflects reality." In smashing that mirror, Wilson's mercurial and sometimes wayward talent has proved itself an immensely important source of theatrical energy. In *The Glad Hand*, which fairly crackles with energy, humour and even good old-fashioned characterization, Wilson has managed to find a way of constructing an absurdism that is socially conscious.

A Note on Heathcote Williams

Heathcote Williams is crucial to any consideration of the theatre since 1968, though his career since the production of his hugely successful

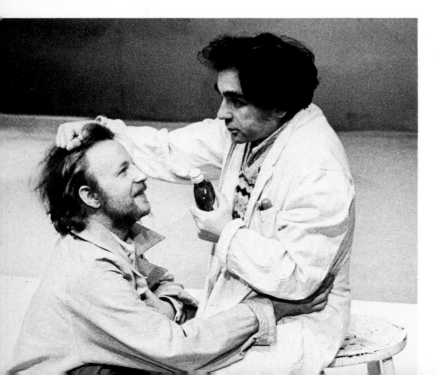

The two schizophrenics – Maurice and Perowne – in Heathcote Williams' aggressive play *AC/DC* seen at the Royal Court in 1969.

AC/DC in 1969 has been fitful, marked by periods of creative silence and public freakout and failing to yield anything remotely comparable with this counter-cultural classic.

AC/DC is a work that embodies both in its form and content many of the neuroses, terrors, joys and fashions of the acid age. Its writer has been likened to Congreve[15] while the play itself has been hailed as an Artaudian fringe classic quite unlike anything else produced in the 1968–73 period. Its unifying mood is one of irresistible physical and psychic energy, and a detailed and aggressive word poetry which occasionally seems to fulfil no dramatic function of any discernible kind. The piece centres on two schizophrenics who encounter three young switched-ons in a strange pin-ball emporium. The threesome is soon separated (two are found to be straights in freaks' clothing) and in the more theatrically stunning second half the remaining character – a black girl, Sadie – becomes embroiled in the often frightening psychic obsessions of Maurice and his factotum, Perowne.

Underlying the impressive, vivid trippy badinage is Williams' fierce belief that individual potential is being drained (in the case of Maurice – literally) by the effects of the constant barrages of undifferentiated media information. It is this assault of 'psychic capitalism' its effects and dangers, that makes *AC/DC* a surprisingly vicarious piece of theatre and one which as an example of 'live' theatre at its unnerving best, creates its own immediate answer to the enveloping horrors of 'media rash'. "Where's the toilet in my brain? How do I flush it?" cries Perowne at one point. In the person of Sadie, Williams creates a vigorous high priestess of inner cleanliness. In a theatrically potent moment Sadie orgiastically destroys Maurice's world of TV movies and rock 'n' roll. At the play's climax she even trepans Perowne – a ritualistic event that disturbingly underlines the almost demonic zeal of this play. (In fact trepanning was for a time a bizarre and deadly cult, particularly in America.)

Williams remains very much a *sui generis* in contemporary theatre: in his love of freaks and loonies he has affinities with the stand-up psychedelic music-hall of Ken Campbell and more formally with writers such as Snoo Wilson and Colin Bennett. *AC/DC* is itself an unrepeated and probably unrepeatable experience.

Trevor Griffiths, David Edgar, Howard Barker:
Three Playwrights into Politics

Trevor Griffiths. Trevor Griffiths is somewhat older than the other writers discussed here, although his creative history begins in 1969 when he was 34. He regards himself primarily as a TV writer, largely because as a Marxist he wishes to reach mass audiences. Nevertheless he is in many ways the most traditional playwright of his kind, a working-class Mancunian keenly concerned with the topic of revolutionary change, its necessity, its problems, its relationship with the often unfulfilled lives of individuals. Griffiths is, above all, a moral writer who believes, in the words of one of his political mentors, Antonio Gramsci, that "It is a revolutionary duty to tell the truth".

Though several of Griffiths' plays have been autobiographically based, the three that stand out in his career to date are the least personalized – *Occupations* (1970), *The Party* (1973) and *Comedians* (1975). The first two are explicitly concerned with the eternal Catch-22 of revolution: how do you create a new order without irredeemably damaging yourself and others, both morally and physically, in the process. *Occupations* was first seen in Manchester, later in London in a production by the Royal Shakespeare Company at their first London studio theatre, The Place, and throughout the country in a production by 7:84. The play is set during the 1920 Turin Fiat motor strike. It opposes two different kinds of revolutionary ideology: the Stalinism of Kabak, a tough, pragmatic Bulgarian agitator who regards the masses as a machine for making revolutions, and Gramsci's commitment to total liberation, based on his intense love of the people "in their particular, detailed, local, individual character". Griffiths spreads the play generously, filling out this basic contrast with other quasi-symbolic personages, such as Kabak's mistress, an aristocrat stricken with cancer, whom he cheats on and finally abandons in a terribly cruel manner, and Valletta, a Fiat executive who illustrates capitalism's ability to adapt to situations which seem to threaten its stability.

The Party, which had the benefit of a prestigious National Theatre production featuring Olivier, Frank Finlay and Denis Quilley, carries on the same theme in a more complex if often excessively naturalistic fashion. (Despite the odd moment of total theatre, *The Party* seems to strain the confines of its own format.) Set in the plush Kensington flat of a trendy TV producer during the Paris riots of 1968, it is concerned with the inability of the British Left to organize itself into a revolutionary weapon. As in *Occupations* the language has an uncompromising didactic tone which is all the more impressive for being direct and uncloyed by theatrical artifice. There are two long accounts of Marxian theory – a revised account by Ford, an LSE lecturer who preaches support for third-world revolutionary groups, and by Tagg, an ageing Glasgow Trotskyist whose analysis is uncompromisingly Bolshevist and contemptuous of the "moral exhaustion" of left-wing intelligentsia. Set cleverly against such theorizing is the living experience of each of the central protagonists: Tagg is stricken with cancer; Shawcross, the producer, by both professional and personal impotence (sexuality is an important factor in the motivation and make-up of Griffiths' characters); while Sloman, an alcoholic writer, is reduced to drunken cynicism, chauvinist snides, and a peculiarly British arid class hatred and Ford, the LSE Marcusian, is

"The Catch-22 of revolution": Trevor Griffiths' *Occupations* in the 7:84 production (1972) with Gavin Richards as the Italian Communist leader, Gramsci.

revealed as something of a lady-killing smoothie. *The Party* is certainly a fascinating play despite its formal shortcomings. Though himself a committed Socialist, Griffiths never falls for easy sermonizing or pat solutions. His numbed producer, Shawcross, ends by giving his younger brother the money he needs to set up in business. An act stemming from Shawcross's obvious distaste for the cold self-sacrifice of Tagg's Revolutionary Socialist Party (obviously modelled on the then Socialist Labour League) it is typically rooted within the complex and often contradictory loyalties of the British working class and its successful disenchanted sons and daughters. Though inspired by and set during the days of May, 1968, *The Party* continues to be topical and pertinent and certainly has a polemical strength far greater than most contemporary plays of political ideas.

First seen in February, 1975, at Nottingham, *Comedians* came to the Old Vic later that year, transferred to the Wyndham's Theatre for a sweet if shortish West End run and somewhat surprisingly (given its Manchester setting and language) wowed both critics and audiences on Broadway, winning for its brilliant young star, Jonathan Pryce, a coveted Tony award.

Like so many genuinely original theatre works, *Comedians* uses form both to embody and reinforce its content. On one level *Comedians* is a play about laughter and about what makes us laugh – comedy as a barometer for the measurement of our joy, of other people's pain, of racial intolerance in which (in the words of its central character, Eddie Waters) "Every joke was a little pellet, a final solution", and even a revolutionary instrument for saying the unsayable and liberating the will. Waters is a former Northern music-hall star who, after fading out of the post-war entertainment scene, now gives evening classes for would-be stand-up comedians. After what is the final session of the term Waters' current pupils are to be accorded a spot down at the local working men's club where their talents will be rigorously analysed by the audience and, more aptly, by a London-based agent of the Comedy Artists and Managers Federation. It was this collaborationist organization that Waters shunned in his performing days, a fact which causes him to be less than optimistic about his lads' chances of success.

For Waters, comedy is ultimately a didactic art: "We work through the laughter, not for it." For Challenor, the agent, it is a means of escape for the audience: "We can't all be Max Bygraves but we can try." But the play's great strength lies in the dialectical process by which Griffiths structures his own internal debate. Waters' best pupil is the sullen, aggressive Gethin whose suddenly changed act is a terrifying explosion of finely tuned hatred, part mime's ferocious integrity, part revenging Jacobean malcontent, part raging, disenfranchised yobbo. And yet Gethin's violent vision of 'ice and fire' is presented in direct contrast to Waters' more humanistic view of progress: "We've gotta get deeper than hate, Gethin. Hate's no help."

Comedians is not without faults. In the third-act confrontation between Waters and Gethin, Waters gives an account of a visit to Buchenwald during a post-war ENSA tour. He tries to explain his disillusionment with 'jokes' and the description ends with the revelation that the place gave him an erection. This latest attempt to relate sexual desire to our basic, darker urges fails not only in terms of character but also dramatically as it seems to be almost immediately swallowed up within the general argument despite its obvious intended shock value. More interestingly because the play contains a second act composed largely of live comedy, Griffiths' intended points fall foul of audiences who may not always oblige by laughing in the right places! For example, Mick's act, the kind of detailed, sympathetic comedy of which Waters approves, actually goes down better with live theatre audiences than it is obviously meant to.

Nevertheless *Comedians* is a remarkable play, a beautifully written, open-ended yet powerful piece of heightened naturalism. It represents Griffiths' last work for the theatre; one can only hope that he intends to write more.

David Edgar. David Edgar was born in 1948 and comes from a fairly conventional, though theatrically inclined, middle-class background. He is the most prolific and in many ways the most representative playwright of his generation. So far he has written 37 stage plays, not counting radio and TV plays and collaborations. Many of these were agitprop pieces performed by the Bradford theatre group General Will on specific social and political issues of the early seventies, for example *Rent – or Caught in the Act*, a Victorian melodrama parody about the Conservative Housing Finance Act and *The National Interest*, on the Industrial Relations Act.

Edgar's other areas of interest have included more complex and some-times over-crammed living documentaries – *The Case of the Workers' Plane*, about Concorde and its workers, and *Events Following the Closure of a Motorcycle Factory*, about the closure of the Norton-Villiers-Triumph factory at Meriden. There are also brilliant parodies, such as *Dick Deterred*, a dynamic musical about Nixon, which was remarkably faithful to its source – *Richard III*; and *Tederella*, a version of the Cinderella story involving Edward Heath and the Common Market Ball. Edgar has also presented more reflective, personalized studies of individuals at odds with the system: *Baby Love*, about a child-stealer who had lost her own baby, and *Excuses, Excuses*, dealing with the thorny motives of a factory arsonist. But since the great success of *Destiny* in 1976 Edgar has divided his time neatly between adaptation, as in *Mary Barnes* and *The Jail Diary of Albie Sachs*, for large subsidized theatres such as the Birmingham Rep, the Royal Court and the RSC, and more dramatized documentary or documentary drama with such touring companies as 7:84 (who did *Wreckers*), Pirate Jenny (*Our Own People*) and Monstrous Regiment (*Teendreams*).

It would be deceptively easy to split Edgar's career into two separate halves, almost using two different clocks: the political activist and the 'serious' dramatist. However, Edgar, who spent some years as a journalist in Bradford, has no qualms about his more obviously political or ephemer-al projects. Indeed, not only did they require a firm grasp of theatrical imagery, economy and factual research, they also represent a good deal that is best about both Edgar's own work and that of his contemporaries: the employment of journalistic criteria as a virtue and not a vice; an ability to tackle public subjects in a serious and uncompromisingly ideological manner; and the development of a brusque, immediate, comic style. Edgar believes that the major problem of his generation's writers is the attempt to merge the psychological drama of naturalism with its emphasis on individual free will and the more rigidly determinist theatre of his own agitprop past. The result would be a dynamic which shows people acting *in relation* to their social situation and exercising some choice. Obviously, as a Socialist, Edgar is also concerned with the quality of that choice.

In *Destiny*, Edgar's most ambitious play to date, he has attempted to create such a dynamic. His central character, Turner, is a man whose personal experience leads him into involvement with ultra-right-wing politics. This experience, however, is also of a business kind for Turner's crucial, personal crisis is the take-over of his small antique shop by a ruthless property conglomerate. Despite an obsession with parasitic worms (the imagery of health and disease runs through the play) Turner's personal make-up is virtually unstated – is he married, gay, divorced? – and with one or two exceptions the action of the play rejects the drawing-room or bedroom setting for the public arena of factory, street, public meeting and picket line.

The play begins in India on Independence Day, 1947, with a collection of army officers drinking scotch and preparing to leave. "Is it true they'll be able to come to England now, to live?" Sergeant Turner asks his Colonel. In the next scene we are in Taddley, a West Midlands town with an unsafe Tory majority and a pending by-election. Colonel Chandler, the town's MP and that old brand of paternalistic Tory also featured in Brenton's *Magnificence* and *Brassneck*, is dead. The nomination goes to his nephew Crosby, the new Tory man, "concerned, humane, constructive, with just the right note of apology in his voice". Meanwhile, Major Rolfe, old-style fire and brimstone, declares his faith in the army and his commitment to the lower middle class: "On all accounts they've been betrayed. Their property no longer secure. Their status in our age increasingly irrelevant. And in the place of national destiny we've given them . . . It's not true we've lost an Empire and haven't found a role. We have a role. As Europe's whipping boy. The one who's far worse off than you are. Kind of awful warning system of the West. And to play that role we must become more shoddy, threadbare, second-rate."

Sergeant Turner, robbed of his business, comes under the influence of the ultra-right party Nation Forward, whose origins are shown in a brilliantly theatrical set piece: a group of people are gathered together and deliberately set up as members of an unspecified left-wing group. Only gradually do we realize that they are members of a British Nazi party gathered to celebrate Hitler's birthday. A Canadian guest rushes in with an evening paper which carries Enoch Powell's infamous 'Rivers of Blood' speech about race, made on the same day on which the scene is set – 20 April, 1968. (Edgar stresses the coincidental nature of the date of these events.) Leaving the assembled jackbooted band the guest declares: "Right, Comrades. For years you have been battering against a bolted door. And now it's open."

One of the play's many strengths is its vast detail, the result of years of painstaking research into right-wing organizations. In a bitter struggle Nation Forward ditches its more populist, socially conscious arm and moves to a position of outright Nazism, world conspiracy and all. Turner becomes Taddley's Nation Forward candidate and is gradually forced into a position of outward anti-Semitism through the tutelage of Nation Forward's Cleaver. The play climaxes with the inter-weaving of two plot

Carol, Cleaver (centre) and Turner, the Nation Forward Party's candidate, in David Edgar's
Destiny – one of the most important political plays of the mid-seventies.

strands: the election and a strike at a local foundry over racial discrimination in piecework and promotion. The strike is led by Khera, the only
Indian representative from the 1947 leaving party. The factory owner
reluctantly employs the Nation Forward party to break the picket line.
Violence ensues, an Indian worker is arrested and deported; the Labour
candidate, despite supporting the strike, refuses to intervene on the
grounds that it would be asking for the law to be broken and not changed,
and the Tory wins the election, Nation Forward picking up 22% of the
vote. At the climax of the play Turner discovers that the firm which took
away his livelihood is owned by Rolfe who is busily engaged in forming a
deal between Nation Forward and Big Business, which obviously parallels
the situation in Germany at the time of Hitler's rise to power.

Destiny suffers in some respects from the problem outlined earlier by
David Hare, insofar as it is open to contrary interpretations according to
the particular prejudices of the individual. It has been accused both of
being a Marxist tract and of being so confused as to be capable of
interpretation as an apologia for fascism. To some extent these points are
valid. The best 'speeches' are often and deliberately put into the mouths of
the characters of whose politics Edgar least approves. Rolfe, for example,
has a profoundly moving monologue over the coffin of his son, killed in
action in Belfast, and Cleaver has a similarly powerful speech about his

own aged uncle, petrified that an Indian temple will be built over his grave. So, too, the weakest characters seem to be the most obviously sympathetic, particularly Clifton, the Labour candidate. Edgar himself has argued that in *Destiny* the plot devices are insufficiently powerful to support the undoubtedly impressive wealth of social detail and verbal power, as if his agitprop sense of construction has led to a skeletal framework for what is in effect an epic play.[16] Indeed, the strike and the election never come close to grabbing our attention from the brilliant scenes involving Nation Forward, while Turner's realization that he has been duped and the Indian worker's comment that British capitalism has a bigger hold over India now than it did in 1947, are never really assimilated into the main thrust of the action. In spite of these flaws *Destiny* is an eloquent and important play.

The history of how the play was written and produced is certainly worth mentioning. It was originally written in 1973 and to start with was five hours long. It was then reduced to a manageable length for the production in 1976 by the RSC at its studio theatre in Stratford. The RSC in the first place turned down the play but this decision was reversed by Ron Daniels who directed it. It was also turned down by the National Theatre, the Birmingham Rep (for whom it was originally written), Nottingham Playhouse, the Royal Court, and the Crucible, Sheffield. Its eventual success brought the play to the RSC's main London theatre, the Aldwych, where it enjoyed the kind of space and audiences that writers such as Edgar and Trevor Griffiths have increasingly courted. Edgar feels that its run at the Aldwych, where it was seen by 22,000 people, had more significance than its showing on television and he believes that it is the middle-class theatre-goers whose 'souls' are most at risk from the forces of the right.[17]

Destiny represents an important development in contemporary theatre insofar as it marks the 'promotion' of radical theatre to suitably large and prestigious settings. This is an event that Edgar, in common with Hare, Brenton and Howard Barker, considers to be of vital importance if the fringe is to consolidate its achievements and writers are to realize their full imaginative potential. *Destiny's* other main importance lies in its complexity. It is the first political play of its kind to come to terms with the attractions of right-wing politics as well as their more obvious shortcomings. Edgar's own researches led him to a committed involvement with the Anti-Nazi League whose active combatting of the National Front on Britain's streets has had an undoubted effect on the (hopefully permanent) decline of Britain's fascist organizations. *Destiny* has itself played a part in that process, while paradoxically it seems that Edgar's most solidly artistic achievement has had the greatest long-term political effect on the society he so obviously longs to improve. Edgar is a prodigious talent, ever willing to learn, highly self-critical and intent on writing plays until he drops. He may well prove to be the most enduring talent of his generation.

Howard Barker.   Howard Barker started as something of a loner. He is a South London-born writer who first became actively interested in the theatre at the advanced age of 22. His first play, *Cheek* (1970), was seen at the Royal Court's Theatre Upstairs, directed by William Gaskill, after having been sent in through the post. Though not a Portable Theatre writer, Barker has forged solid links with several organizations – the Theatre Upstairs, the Open Space (where his *Alpha Alpha* and *Claw* were produced) and, most recently with the RSC's Warehouse, which has so far tackled three of his later works: *That Good Between Us* (1977), *The Hang of the Gaol* (1978) and *The Loud Boy's Life* (1980). Additionally, *Stripwell* (1975), *Fair Slaughter* (1978) and *The Love of a Good Man* (1980) were all seen in the Royal Court's main downstairs theatre.[18] Though Barker has never been a commercially-orientated dramatist, he is the author of three screenplays, including the award-winning *Aces High*.

Barker is in many ways the Peter Pan of his generation. While other writers have toned down their early sense of moral outrage and class hatred, Barker's plays continue to carry an intense, emotional impact and a deep and often unfocused sense of political and sexual antagonism. His style is an energetic mix of comedy and declamatory phrase-making, though in *Stripwell* he demonstrated his ability to capture the more static exchanges of the middle classes. Nevertheless his sympathies seem to lie with working-class waifs like the Scot Billy McPhee in *That Good Between Us* and Biledew, the doomed pimp in *Claw*; with old men like Gocher in *Fair Slaughter*; and, most intriguingly, with figures of moral and political ambiguity who have moved downwards or upwards in the social spectrum.

Barker's vision of contemporary society, like Brenton's in *Magnificence*, is of a huge con trick which encourages the more individualistic members of the working class to exploit each other in terms of crime and reaction: the nightmare society of spies and counter-spies that is *That Good Between Us*, the exploits of the Kray-style gangster twins in *Alpha Alpha*. Like Brenton and Edgar, Barker is an avid lampoonist and his victims have included Sir Francis Chichester, Heath, the Duke of Windsor, Enoch Powell and Lord Shinwell. In more recent works, however, he has demonstrated a more ambitious grasp of narrative, setting and character-ization, while managing, through a kind of stylistic collage, to retain a good deal of the old ferocity and sexual aggression. For all his bile, he is another ambiguous writer, disgusted with the present iniquities of society and yet both respectful of old-world virtue and seemingly convinced that a great deal of humanity's problems rest in the intractable sexual warfare which permeates his plays. The undoubted confusion results in a some-what inevitable tendency to attack the waverer and the compromiser as much and even more than the hated extremist. Labour peers who 'sold out' to the revolution abound, as do Labour police chiefs, women prime ministers and a drunken home secretary. Like Kurtz in Conrad's *Heart of Darkness*, many of Barker's establishment figures are would-be civilizers stalked by violence and madness. Cooper, the prison governor turned arsonist in *The Hang of the Gaol* is a classic example.

At his best Barker can compose immensely powerful language, particularly for those characters who burn with a sense of ignorance and helplessness. His gift for comic invention and inversion is similarly impressive. Biledew, the four-eyed diminutive pimp in *Claw* is a marvellous antithesis to Osborne's angry young man Jimmy Porter. Barker's ability to create startling *coups de théâtre* is almost unrivalled among his peers: the climax of *Stripwell* in which a young tearaway shoots the anti-hero judge after a seemingly endless moment of indecision; the seance on the field of Passchendaele in *The Love of a Good Man* and the violent conflagration between two civil servants of the opposite sex in *The Hang of the Gaol*.

Barker's main shortcomings are his inability to write parts for women that do not reverberate with what seems to be an imported sense of male sexual antagonism, and his tendency to load his more morally and politically dubious creations with a lot of leaden and barely credible self-apology and irony. So too *That Good Between Us* creates a given nightmare world of the future which, for all its power, teeters on the edge of sci-fi fantasy, while *Claw's* rivetting final act rests for its very existence on the bizarre proposition that the British Establishment keeps open extermination camps staffed by such notables as an ex-terrorist psychopath and a former hangman's assistant. It certainly seems that in Barker's plays virtue and vice stalk together. Political confusion leads to a good

The Hang of the Gaol by Howard Barker. Nicholas le Prevost in the 1978 production at The Warehouse.

deal of easy moralizing but also accounts for the undoubted intensity of their vision of social and personal injustice. The comedy, though occasionally prone to the puerile, is more often deft and startling, while in a theatrical landscape often tending to sedateness and aridity, Barker can create colossal, even unforgettable confrontations out of thin air.

Stephen Poliakoff and Barrie Keeffe: *The School of Inarticulacy*

The increased importance of youth culture in society, coupled with the concern among writers of all social backgrounds for the more deprived sections of the population, have led to a number of plays about the frustrations of youth, be it young blacks harassed by the police, pop-mad assistants in a Midlands supermarket or school-leavers faced with the prospect of unemployment.

Stephen Poliakoff.   Stephen Poliakoff, born in 1952, educated at Westminster and Cambridge (which he left, like David Hare, in his second year), had a brief, precocious contact with Portable Theatre on the multi-compositional *Lay By*, a study of contemporary attitudes to pornography, written by six authors working under a process of collective isolation in 1971. However, Poliakoff's most important contributions to theatre came later and his most memorable creations are scenes of urban disintegration and adolescent claustrophobia. *Hitting Town* (1975), a sophisticated study of a brother and sister on the town in concrete jungle land, is not only intriguing for its incestuous overtones but for its splendidly vibrant images of modern consumerist convenience-orientated society *in extremis*: in a Wimpy bar a tomato ketchup container is cut open to reveal revolting contents which run to cigarette ends, half a sardine and a tooth!

Poliakoff is particularly adept at illustrating the elemental nature of youthful disquiet, its potential for nihilism and morbidity. (In *Shout Across the River* (1978) the brother of the central character Christine, herself on a voluntary starvation kick, has an amusing obsession with disaster and even seems pleased when he ends up in a hospital bed after being mugged.) In *City Sugar* (1975), a Leicester DJ, who alternates between self-disgust at the failure of his sixties' idealism and contempt for his audience, confronts a hostile but rather emotionless shop assistant, Nicola, after a bizarre radio contest, part of which has involved the building of dolls in the shape of a pop artist. Nicola and her friend fill the doll with frozen food and in another exchange the friend, Susan, describes in typically gory detail the soggy contents of a fused refrigerator. As in other of his plays, *City Sugar*, though wittily and intelligently written, presents a fascinating balance of inarticulate and articulate forces: the snappy DJ Leonard Brazil and the sullen, recalcitrant teenager, Nicola.

Poliakoff remains an intriguing figure in contemporary theatre, not least because he has shown a marked and increasingly uncommon interest in characterization for its own sake: in *Shout Across the River*, the creation of Mrs Forsythe, a mother in early middle age with an enveloping terror of social intercourse and a problem teenage daughter with whom she strikes up a bizarre and passionate relationship, is marvellously sensitive. It is also convincingly placed within the familiar Poliakoff terrain of South London flat, cavernous comprehensive, soulless disco and depopulated ice cream parlour.

Barrie Keeffe. Barrie Keeffe was born in East Ham in 1945 and has no doubt benefited from the social contact his background and career (sports reporter, factory worker, grave digger, etc) has afforded him. His most notable achievement to date is his trilogy *Gimme Shelter* (1977) which comprises three short plays: *Gem*, *Gotcha* and *Getaway*, all of which were produced originally at the Soho Poly. Keeffe's forte is the depiction of the more socially deprived youth of the London area; in *Gotcha* a hitherto uninspiring under-achiever at a large comprehensive school holds two teachers, and later the headmaster, in terror with the aid of a lighted cigarette and an exposed motorcycle petrol tank. This short piece of enormous dramatic force and intense moral outrage is flanked in the trilogy by two plays, *Gem* and *Getaway*, set in different years during an annual cricket match involving a London insurance firm. In these plays Keeffe is particularly adept at capturing the gnawing hunger beneath the banter of clerkish conversation and the insidious way in which vague political unease can be assimilated or deflected by the forces of conformity and small ambition.

At his best Keeffe is a powerful, good-natured writer capable of composing moving pleas on behalf of those unassured representatives of society commonly ignored by contemporary theatre. Nevertheless that potency is threatened by his failings, not least of which are a tendency to sentimentalize his characters (particularly the representatives of old Cockney values) and, more recently, a tendency towards a political explicitness which breaks up the texture of his assured characterization and fails to convince, largely because political analysis is obviously not one of the writer's strengths. Thus *Sus* (1979) – in which a black suspect is bullied by two racist policeman who suspect him of a particularly brutal wife-murder – is set against the recent Conservative election victory out of which it makes much theatrical capital. However, it makes no attempt to analyse the reasons for such an eventuality, while the piece is further hampered dramatically by the blatant and almost unrelieved antagonism with which both policemen view their black charge.[19]

More generally Keeffe's writing suffers from the constraints of his chosen form – naturalism – particularly in the over-regular use of jokes and anecdotes to prop up the dramatic situation, and by the offloading of articulate philosophizings into the mouths of seemingly inarticulate characters. In *Gotcha*, however, the dramatic situation created just the

A comprehensive headmaster under threat of immolation in *Gotcha*, part of the *Gimme Shelter* trilogy by Barrie Keeffe.

right amount of intense self-awareness to propel the pent-up rage of the school student, providing an apt and effective correlative for his sudden articulacy.

Despite all their many differences, all the playwrights discussed above inhabit very much the same theatrical universe. Bernard Levin, explaining his sudden resignation as *Sunday Times* drama critic, felt that the common quality was "... the relentless negativity with which they are suffused".[20] For Levin these writers had failed in the first duty of the playwright: to reflect the pre-occupations of his society. In so doing their art denied life.

But the question remains open. These writers' plays are almost obsessively concerned with violence, with social injustice, with betrayed and disappointed hopes, with the darker side of life. Are these themes a true reflection of Britain in the throes of post-colonial decline, do they not point to something rotten in the state of the United Kingdom? Or are they merely the psychopathic fantasizings of a group of gifted neurotics? The latter cannot explain why so many of our best writers individually reflect life so critically, nor why they are so important and influential.

And yet, the writers of today face problems of subject matter and technique as great as at any time in the theatre's history. It seems already true that apprehensions about social inequality are inadequate by themselves to sustain and nourish both audiences and artists. In some ways these writers can be seen to have come full circle in the past fifteen years. Perhaps once again the time is ripe for playwrights to explore new subjects and new styles (perhaps most specifically with better characterization) through a search for new audiences?

References

1 David Hare in an interview with Ann McFerran *Time Out* No. 285, 29 August 1975.
2 Howard Brenton in an interview in *Theatre Quarterly* No. 17, 1975.
3 W. Stephen Gilbert *Plays and Players*, June 1978.
4 Quoted in *Time Out* No. 209, 1 March 1974.
5 David Hare in an interview with Steve Grant *Time Out* No. 418, 7 April 1978. (See also introduction to *Licking Hitler*, Faber, 1978).
6 All quotes from plays are from the published editions.
7 John Peter *The Sunday Times*.
8 Charles Marowitz *Plays and Players*, September 1976.
9 Peter Ansorge *Disrupting the Spectacle* p. 3 (Pitman 1975).
10 David Hare in an interview with Steve Grant *op. cit.*
11 Howard Brenton and David Hare in the preface to *Brassneck* (Eyre Methuen, 1974).
12 David Hare in an interview with Steve Grant *op. cit.*
13 Snoo Wilson in an interview with Michael Coveney *Time Out* No. 502, 30 November 1979.
14 Peter Ansorge *op. cit.* p. 17.
15 By William Gaskill in a radio broadcast, quoted by John Russell Taylor in *The Second Wave* (Eyre Methuen, 1971).
16 David Edgar in an interview in *Theatre Quarterly* No. 33, 1979.
17 David Edgar in an interview with Steve Grant *Time Out* No. 371, 6 May 1977.
18 *The Love of a Good Man* was a visiting production presented by the Oxford Playhouse.
19 At the time of writing Keeffe's latest play *Bastard Angel* was enjoying a successful run at The Warehouse.
20 Bernard Levin *The Sunday Times*, 25 November 1979.

10 Subversion at Lunchtime

Or business as usual?

Rosalind Asquith

"Nothing so quickly dispels one's sense of reality as a daubed and bedizened actor standing four feet from one's face and declaiming right over one's head."

Kenneth Tynan, 1962[1]

"Big buildings aren't necessary . . . theatre can happen anywhere."

Fred Proud, 1973[2]

The anti-naturalism of much of the fringe theatre of the late sixties influenced not only the texts of the day, and the styles of performance; it influenced attitudes to the audience and to the playing space, orthodox views of the theatre as an art-form, and of the theatre as a leisure activity. How much the new fringe represented a break with the traditional theatre or how much it was merely peripheral, is a perennial question which is illuminated by the diversity of motives behind the establishment of one of the most distinctive of fringe initiatives: lunchtime theatre.

The original intentions were numerous – from the blatantly commercial impulse to showcase the work of new writers and performers in circumstances that were relatively painless economically, to the much more radical motive that, by presenting plays at an unusual time of day, one was breaking through one of the paradigm conventions of Western theatre. In turn it was thought that this break-through would have numerous 'fall-out' consequences. Firstly, because of its accessibility and its cheapness, it would attract ordinarily disinterested audiences. Secondly, by inserting entertainment into the working day, the bourgeois categorization of time into 'work' and 'leisure' would be disrupted. This in turn would lead to subversion of the whole conventional way of thinking about the world. Thirdly, by presenting theatre in a new environment – new time of day, new space, new audience – and by combining the consumption of plays with the consumption of lunch, one made theatre into a completely different social activity in which the old theatrical rules and petrified conventions could be discarded.

In fact, reality has not quite lived up to these ambitious objectives. Lunchtime theatre has provided, and continues to provide, an invaluable outlet and showcase for 'resting' actors and new playwrights. But it has rarely become the launching pad to the West End and stardom. Meanwhile, the expansion of the evening fringe theatres in London in the early and mid-seventies – significantly after the founding of such pioneering lunchtime theatres as the Ambiance, the Basement and the Soho Poly – has competed with the lunchtime theatres and undercut their reason for existence.

On the other hand, the original radical intentions now seem more than a little idealistic. Nevertheless lunchtime plays did encourage the more general development of what has been called the 'cartoon-style' of writing and performance: a racy, no-frills, shorthand method of writing and direction made all the more immediate by the extremely close proximity of the actors to the audience in many lunchtime venues. Indeed, because of the conditions of proximity, small space, minimum of time and economy of means, the lunchtime theatre has developed a new genre: the intense confessional monologue. This is, perhaps, the theatrical equivalent of the twentieth century novel's technique of stream of consciousness. At any rate, it is able to mix the naturalistic and the surrealistic (through the fantasies of the monologuer) without awkwardness. Unfortunately, though capable of adaptation for television or radio, such a form seems set apart from the rest of theatre. Only David Halliwell has attempted to take its basic premise – the non-objectivity of the 'real' world – further, and his experiments in 'multi-viewpoint' drama must now be considered as interesting, if limited.

Perhaps lunchtime theatre's position in the theatre world was always ambiguous. Nowadays, in a worsening economic climate and with threats of cuts in the arts looming, its position seems even more precarious than ever. In 1973 there were as many as ten regular London venues. Although the city's midday theatre-goers could, in January 1979, have seen a video performance by Action Space at the Drill Hall, an anti-nuclear energy season at the Almost Free, an engrossing study of three generations of Australian women and Alan Pope's witty and inspiring *Double Exposure* (about growing up gay) at Putney's Head Theatre, an anthology of Dorothy Parker's writings at the King's Head in Islington, or an entertainment based on P. G. Wodehouse's stories at the Young Vic – by the end of that year there were only two regular lunchtime theatres in London, one of which, the King's Head, was housing only visiting productions while saving its own shows for the evening. (The other was the Soho Poly.)

More damningly, lunchtime theatre was never able to take root outside London. At least in the late sixties and the early seventies there had been a number of attempts in most of Britain's larger cities to establish lunchtime theatres, usually with their own bohemian ambiance. By the end of the seventies these attempts had petered out and lunchtime theatre was confined to London. Indeed, the suspicion that lunchtime theatre is more a market phenomenon – as a cheap proving-ground for new theatrical talent necessitating a large army of unemployed theatre-workers (such as is only available in London) – than a distinctly new form of theatre, is borne out by the experience of probably the only truly successful lunchtime theatre outside London, the Pool Theatre in Edinburgh. (Full name, The Other Pool Synod Hall.)

The Pool.   The Pool ran from 1971 to 1974 in which time, as well as presenting productions by visiting companies of the calibre of Portable Theatre, John Bull Puncture Repair Kit, Bradford College of Art, the Ken Campbell Road Show, Pip Simmons and the Welfare State, it presented its own programme of lunchtime shows, premiering new plays by writers like David Edgar and Richard Crane and productions by Lindsay Kemp. But though the Pool maintained a genuinely experimental policy it had, in fact, been set up with the help of John Gray, Chief Assistant at BBC Radio Scotland, who was to become its chairman. The proximity of Glasgow allowed the Pool to draw on a much larger 'pool' of unemployed actors and theatre-workers than other regional cities; while the nature of the Scottish entertainment industry (including theatre, television, radio and 'club' entertainment) and its comparative separation and isolation from its English counterpart, enabled the Pool to act as a showcase for talent. Its survival was additionally helped by the large bohemian sub-culture in Edinburgh and the yearly bonanza of the Edinburgh Festival Fringe.

The Pool, in fact, combined the best of both the radical and entrepreneurial facets of lunchtime theatre, though as Allen Wright commented in *The Scotsman*: "Emanuel and his partner, John Cumming, have stocked the Pool with a wide range of entertainment. Even if it is seldom avant-garde, it is always enterprising."[3] For three years the Pool staggered from financial crisis to financial crisis and its death-blow only came when the owners of its building forced them to leave prior to the redevelopment of the site (i.e. its destruction). By that time no one was prepared to devote the necessary energy to re-establish it in other premises and the venture folded. The experience of the Pool illustrates the thesis that lunchtime theatre is a particular theatrical species which requires a habitat only to be found in London.

The origins of London's lunchtime theatre scene are shrouded in a certain amount of hazy recollection. Though David Halliwell and David Calderisi, who founded Quipu at the New Arts Theatre Club in 1966, are generally taken to be the originators, Halliwell himself credits the departure to an Australian duo calling itself Theatrescope, which had set up some lunchtime performances the previous year at the Little Theatre Club in St Martin's Lane. Certainly, by the end of 1968, Ed Berman had established

Inter-Action's Ambiance Lunch Hour Theatre Club in Queensway (it transferred four years later to the Almost Free Theatre in Piccadilly), while Fred Proud and Verity Bargate had set up the Soho Poly near Oxford Circus. Within a few years the King's Head was regularly presenting outside productions at lunchtime, while most of the evening fringe theatres across the city occasionally presented one-off productions or lunchtime seasons. (These included the Open Space, the Half Moon, the Orange Tree at Richmond and the ICA.) Nevertheless it is the earliest established theatres which have been most successful and enduring.

Ambiance. Ed Berman's Ambiance Lunch Hour Theatre Club quickly gained a formidable reputation for adventurous new work. Berman and his assistant on this Inter-Action project, Naftali Yavin – who was director of The Other Company from 1968 until his death in 1972 – sought to illuminate and analyse the social conventions which so rigidly structure everyday life in the Western world and which straitjacket personality into a series of stereotypical roles. Their ideas about 'environmental' theatre and the use of theatre to develop individual expression through such a critique has obvious affinities both with the development of Inter-Action's

David Rudkin's *The Filth Hunt* (1973) concerning a self-styled Pornography Commission in league with the Devil, seen at the Almost Free Theatre, which has played host to a large number of excellent lunchtime productions.

community work and with the radical motivations behind lunchtime theatre – that by presenting theatre at lunchtime one was already breaking through social conventions. Early Ambiance productions were typified by a painstaking concern for language and the absence within the plays of a social reality – a quality they share with the 'confessional monologue' genre and an obvious reaction against the dominant naturalism of the day. They included John Arden's bizarre monologue *Squire Jonathan*, Ed Berman's *Nudist Campers Grow and Grow* and James Saunders' *Dog Accident*. In each case the way the play was staged actively involved and included the audience.

Yavin further explored this way of working with his evening productions at the Almost Free, which included Peter Handke's audience-offending piece and James Saunders' *Games* and *After Liverpool*, although recently Inter-Action's approach has been somewhat different. Berman maintains a fruitful artistic relationship with Tom Stoppard. In fact, his lunchtime play *Dirty Linen*, first seen at the Almost Free, was subsequently developed and became one of Stoppard's most astonishing successes, enjoying a prolonged West End run. Stoppard's delight in juggling the raw materials of the English language was actually revealed at its purest and funniest in his 1972 lunchtime play for Inter-Action's Dogg's Troupe – anagrammatically titled *Doggs Our Pet* – a dialogue of beautifully constructed gibberish. Of course, Stoppard's pieces are primarily entertainment (in the non-pejorative sense) rather than deep brow-beating searches for meaning in contemporary life.

Ambiance at the Almost Free has also been something of a guardian of minority rights, with seasons constructed around themes such as sex and consciousness, rights and campaigns, and an 'anti-nuclear' season that included a good deal of street theatre. Indeed, Ambiance's gay and women's seasons, which included work by writers Pam Gems and Michelene Wandor and directors Gerald Chapman, Drew Griffiths and Su Todd, not only lent some valuable thematic coherence but were instrumental in the development of those areas of theatre. It is also the only theatre in Britain to stage John Arden and Margaretta D'Arcy's epic *Non-Stop Connolly Show*, in a cycle of lunchtime workshop performances. The Almost Free's importance as a platform and resources centre for minority groups can easily be undervalued.

Although redevelopment has deprived Ambiance of the Almost Free for 1979/80, they are continuing in different venues (initially Action Space) and director Anthony Matheson intends to explore further the structural possibilities of the telescoped theatrical form by introducing a series of workshop-produced plays in which a writer will have free rein to choose a cast, improvise with them and direct the emerging work. It's an open, ambitious and potentially illuminating approach, which has its roots in over a decade of experimenting. (It is also reminiscent of Fred Proud's

1973 Soho Poly season.) The Almost Free Theatre, incidentally, has a box-office policy which demands merely that its customers pay what they can – anything upwards of a penny. As it has turned out, idealism has been a trifle too synonymous with poverty, and they are currently reconsidering the policy. The Ambiance troupe also tries to shift the odds by touting for business, street-crier style, before the performance – though that is perhaps an anachronism from the days when it was thought easy to attract the office-worker into the lunchtime theatre.

The Soho Poly.   By comparison with Ambiance's experimentalism, the Soho Poly appears almost staid at first sight. Nevertheless it probably rivals Berman's group in the significance of its contribution. Proud left in 1975 but, under the artistic direction of Verity Bargate, the Soho Poly maintains the reputation as a writers' theatre that it developed through the sympathetic atmosphere it provided for the young writers of the fringe boom. It has also been instrumental in changing working patterns within the theatre, drawing the writer into the production process. Proud's 1973 season with director Chris Parr is an illustration of this development. Proud deliberately set up the complete season with Parr, six actors and a group of writers to produce a series of lunchtime shows with the diverting titles of *Come, Fun, Coal, True Life* and *Grabberwitch.* Working cooperatively, Proud's scheme was an impressive attempt to help unestablished writers find their feet both by removing their sense of isolation and by allowing them to test their writing ideas constantly against the reality of acting and the stage. (Only one of the five writers, David Mowat, was preceded by his reputation.)

The Soho Poly's powers of survival make it a fascinating test case, since venues which produce their own lunchtime shows as opposed to renting out their space are now limited to Ambiance, Richmond's Orange Tree (in the summer only) and the Poly itself. In 1972/73 Bargate and Proud received a grant of £3,000 from the Arts Council. With this they premiered around thirty plays, paying the actors only £5 each and the writers a commission of £50. Idealistic arguments were still raging on the fringe as to the pros and cons of state subsidy for work which aimed, in some respects at least, to be revolutionary. (Indeed, actors at some other lunchtime theatres did even worse than those at the Poly, sometimes even paying their own fares to the theatre and playing for free.) The lunchtime theatres, however, attracted not only young, aspiring actors but also some of the more established ones, mainly because, through its very format, its intimacy and informality, lunchtime theatre is the showcase *par excellence* for the actor. Julia Foster, David Warner and Colin Blakely all worked at the Soho Poly during the 1972/73 season.

Today at the Soho Poly, things have changed. Now an Equity-recognized theatre, it pays above the minimum rate to actors from an annual grant of £30,000. Yet twice that sum is needed to comfortably produce fifteen plays

A South African bar re-created at the Soho Poly for *Soul of the White Ant* (1976) by Snoo Wilson, directed by Dusty Hughes.

a year and the plays they do produce are budgeted on 3.5 actors per show. Nowadays the writers come off worst – £150 Royalty Supplement from the Arts Council plus perhaps £30 from the box office – and the Theatre Writers' Union is mounting a campaign similar to Equity's earlier efforts. Better treatment of writers would be a fitting outcome of Proud's early initiatives. His work has certainly helped writers to gain a more influential role in rehearsals as well as in casting and choice of director. The Soho Poly has premiered work by writers of the stature of Howard Brenton, Snoo Wilson, Barrie Keeffe (see Chapter 9) and Pam Gems. But paradoxically the Theatre Writers' Union's campaign against self-exploitation may limit the number of new plays presented at lunchtime. The Arts Council, which must provide most of the money, is not totally committed to new writing. More particularly, it views lunchtime theatre with fairly reluctant indulgence because lunchtime plays, being short, are not seen as giving 'value for money' while audiences are restricted by the small seating capacities of the venues. The somewhat patronizing view that lunchtime theatre is of value only as a kind of Research & Development department for the rest of theatre seems to be more and more detectable.

And yet the showcasing of new talent, particularly writers, at the Soho Poly, the King's Head and other lunchtime theatres, seems to be its most lasting achievement. Certainly, of the dream of engendering a new theatre audience, little remains. The average cross-section of audiences is unrepentantly theatrical: actors, agents and TV talent scouts account for most of the audience though tourists, particularly American, and perhaps 10% locals are also present.

Lunchtime theatre is, in fact, a tributary of the theatre world that is almost unique to Britain (in New York, for instance, you'd have to pay upwards of $1,000 simply to rent the space) and to London where it is fed by the frustrations of the hundreds of unemployed actors in the capital, and the dissatisfaction of more successful thespians who are otherwise kicking their heels in run-of-the-mill West End shows or routine TV jobs.

In a world where every private hopes to be a general — one of Western society's most insidious temptations — the overcrowded and competitive theatrical profession is one of the most vulnerable. But, since the early days of Halliwell's 'multi-viewpoint' drama at Quipu, and its identification as a platform for reconsidering short or rarely performed works, lunchtime theatre has overcome its lack of a coherent policy through the vital breaks it has given to an endless list of emergent playwrights.

References

1 Kenneth Tynan *Right and Left* (Longman, 1967).
2 Fred Proud in an interview with Peter Ansorge *Plays and Players*, June 1973.
3 Allen Wright *The Scotsman*, 7 July 1972.

11 Showcasing the Fringe

The venues

Malcolm Hay

The work of the new theatre groups of the late sixties and early seventies was never designed to be played in conventional theatres. Whatever the differences in aims, ideology, methods of work, and styles of performance between the groups, they were all actively concerned with seeking new audiences. And these audiences were not likely to be drawn from the regular theatre-going public of the time.

The form of their shows was in no way suited to the limitations of traditional staging. While some groups moved totally outside the bounds of conventional theatre, performing outdoors in the streets or in 'found' environments, for others the prime requirement was an adaptable and flexible performance space so that the relationship between actors and audience could be varied according to the nature of specific shows.

The many small theatre venues that sprang up during this time were a logical and necessary outcome of the activities of the touring groups. Twelve years on it is easy to forget how radical a departure this was from the standard theatrical practice of the sixties. The fringe came into being as a result of the ideas and efforts of performers, directors, and playwrights who were not associated with any of the existing theatres or permanent theatre buildings.

The shortage of venues for new groups like The People Show, Pip Simmons, and Portable Theatre was chronic. But in the space of only three or four years, between 1969 and 1973, a large number of small, independent theatres came into existence, often taking over disused premises or spaces such as the back rooms in pubs and converting them into rudimentary theatres. The extent and rapidity of their growth in London can be charted through the theatre listings in *Time Out*. At the end of 1968 there were fewer than a dozen such venues – they included the Ambiance, the Drury Lane Arts Lab, the ICA, the Open Space Theatre, and Oval House. In 1980 *Time Out*'s section on 'Fringe Shows and Events' regularly lists between 40 and 50 venues each week.

Casualties have been heavy. Many of these small theatres, run on a shoestring without Arts Council subsidy or any other grant, survived only for a year or two. Those which have survived fulfilled two main functions. They provided a platform for the work of the new touring groups; and, in some cases, they also mounted their own productions, providing an outlet for new writers like Snoo Wilson and Howard Brenton, who had already cut their teeth on the touring circuit with Portable Theatre.

One of the most influential figures in the early days of the fringe was an American, Jim Haynes. Although he was neither an actor, nor a director, nor a writer, his impact as an impresario, whose tastes and sympathies coincided with the broad 'alternative' cultural movement of the late sixties, was immense. In fact he was well in advance of the times. In the early sixties he owned and ran a bookshop in Edinburgh, and organized in the basement performances of plays followed by a discussion. In 1962, together with Terry Lane and an actor, John Malcolm, he took over an old building that had once been one of the most famous brothels in the city and converted it into a small theatre.

The Traverse. The Traverse Theatre – so named because the stage literally traversed the auditorium, dividing the audience into two blocks – could hold only sixty people, and many of the theatre's economic problems throughout the sixties were directly attributable to the fact that the income which could be generated from the box-office was so small.

For the first 14 months Haynes was technically Chairman of the Traverse Theatre Club, with Lane as artistic director, though Haynes exerted a strong influence over artistic policy. After the opening year, in which they put on a staggering total of 22 plays, Haynes took over as artistic director, though still not directing any of the productions himself. By the time he resigned and left the Traverse, in 1966, the theatre had survived, somewhat precariously, the difficult early years.

The history since then is one of successive artistic directors building on the foundation of new British and foreign avant-garde drama that Haynes and Lane had introduced. Gordon McDougall (from 1966–68) instituted the practice of mounting Traverse productions at larger venues elsewhere in the city – a clear sign of the financial limitations involved in remaining in the original building. Under his successor, Max Stafford-Clark, the Traverse moved to new premises, doubling thereby the potential audience and also obtaining a far more flexible performance space. The period under Max Stafford-Clark (from 1968–70) coincided with the growth of the fringe theatre movement in the rest of the country. He interspersed a steady stream of British and world premieres with visits from many of the new performance groups, but perhaps the most significant innovation was the foundation of the Traverse Theatre Workshop Company, a small group of actors and musicians who, with Stafford-Clark as director, occupied the old Traverse building as a base for some three years and developed there a series of shows which toured Britain and Europe, while Mike Rudman took over the reins at the Traverse Theatre itself.

Rudman's time there was a period of consolidation — and far greater financial stability than ever before — with a much wider spectrum of plays being shown. Mike Ockrent (1973–75) narrowed the main focus of the work again by concentrating predominantly on foreign plays, but the most distinct and positive shift in policy has been Chris Parr's deliberate emphasis since 1976 on the work of Scottish playwrights. The Traverse has now become essentially a writers' theatre and Parr hopes to confine visiting productions to a short season of some six to eight weeks each year. The evident public support for this new direction has resulted in larger potential audiences than the theatre, which holds 105–110 comfortably, can cater for. A move to a larger auditorium is now under discussion.

The Arts Lab.   Two years after leaving the Traverse, Jim Haynes launched in London another venture which, although very short-lived, was to characterize the general values and ideals of the counter-culture of the late sixties more definitively than anywhere else. The Drury Lane Arts Lab remained open for only 21 months, from January 1968 to October 1969, but during that time it offered a platform for many theatre groups who were subsequently to have a major influence on the shape of alternative theatre.

The Arts Lab housed a variety of events, from films to multi-media shows to theatre. The informal atmosphere also ensured that it served as a meeting-place, and as a magnet for casual visitors (or sightseers) who didn't necessarily intend to see any of the shows. Informality was the keynote and this extended to the programming. In December 1968 the listing in *Time Out* for the Arts Lab carried the following advice: "The Arts Lab programme appears to be a mixture of chaos and chance and details should be obtained by phone for any one evening."[1]

To some extent the casualness and occasional chaos was the result of

Pip Simmons' typically energetic *Do It!* based on Jerry Rubin's book, at The Traverse (1971).

running a relatively large operation, which offered many diverse events, on a shoestring. But it was probably also a conscious reaction against the idea of 'professionalism'. With theatre the Arts Lab operated an open door policy: companies and groups were welcomed in without much regard for any 'objective' judgement about the standard of their work. The consequence was a heady mixture of shows of many types – many of them pretentious or poorly performed. At the same time Haynes' methods enabled groups like Pip Simmons, The People Show, and others to develop their ideas on a public platform, and above all in a sympathetic environment. The Drury Lane Arts Lab was to serve as a model, and indeed an inspiration, for the many small arts labs which opened throughout the country in the next few years.

Oval House.   Apart from the Arts Lab, Oval House in Kennington was the only venue in London in 1968 or early 1969 that regularly presented the work of the new theatre groups. Like the Arts Lab it furnished the groups with a space to perform in and freely allowed them the right to experiment and the right to fail, without the pressures engendered in mainstream theatres by the lack of immediate and constant critical and public approval. Oval House differed, however, in one important respect. Whereas Jim Haynes had created an art-house which epitomized the ideals of the counter-culture of the time, Peter Oliver (administrator of Oval House until 1972) laid down a much broader base of activities, most notably the workshops – in dance, theatre, music, mime, clowning, and much more besides. These workshops, in which amateurs would often work alongside professional performers, embodied in practice the ideal of everyone being a potential artist. Oval House was, and is, an arts lab in the true sense of the word, providing outlets for people to do things themselves and offering a valid alternative to conventional, consumer-oriented theatres where all you can do is go and watch a show.

Peter Oliver had been appointed way back in 1961 as Warden of Oval House, then a sports-orientated Boys' Club. In accordance with a "firm belief in the usefulness of the arts and their relevance to young people",[2] he converted the old football gym into a theatre which could seat 120 on moveable rostra. A chapel upstairs became a second, smaller theatre. A room containing a boxing-ring was transformed into a dance studio (in the early days the dance workshops shared the space with an energetic weight-training club). A youth drama group was set up, run by teachers and out-of-work actors, and funded by the Drama Department of the Inner London Education Authority.

When Jim Haynes' Arts Lab folded, Oval House – which had already housed shows by many of the new groups – became the natural 'home' for Freehold, The People Show, and many others to migrate to. The place switched from being largely a centre for educational drama to become a complete arts centre. It is difficult now to name a group of any standing that *hasn't* appeared there, but Peter Oliver also offered other invaluable services and support. His most farsighted decision was to allow groups to rehearse at Oval House free of charge, provided that they performed the resulting show at least once at the Oval.

Oliver's departure in 1973 to work as an actor with the Pip Simmons Company was partly motivated by his feeling that he was in danger of "... being institutionalized as a figurehead, as 'the father of the fringe'." Oval House itself has successfully avoided that fate. The aims have remained effectively unchanged, with the result that it is now the stamping-ground for a new generation of groups and performers, while the major, long-established companies appear more and more often in larger theatres.

A venue like Oval House was precious in 1969, when a host of English companies – Ken Campbell, Berkoff's London Theatre Group, Pip Simmons, Freehold, The La Mama Repertory Company, The People Show – were eking out a living (and developing their work) by making regular trips to appear at the Mickery Theatre in Amsterdam. Its enlightened manager and director, Ritsaert ten Cate, rivals Oliver and Haynes in the creative contribution he made towards the growth of fringe theatre in Britain. At the very least he was instrumental in keeping many of the groups alive early on. Activities at the Mickery expanded to include three-month residential workshop experiments – groups were provided with accommodation and expenses while they worked on a new show, without any pressure to come up with a production for the Mickery itself.
The Theatre Upstairs. In London, the Royal Court opened its small studio theatre, The Theatre Upstairs, in 1969, converting a large room at the top of the building which had formerly doubled as a rehearsal room and a club. The Theatre Upstairs differs in almost every respect from Oval House. It has rarely housed visiting productions or the work of the touring groups, although the historic *Come Together* festival in autumn 1969, which occupied both the new upstairs auditorium and the main house downstairs, served as a temporary showcase for many of the new companies. Instead, it has built a reputation on a policy of putting on new plays by writers like Howard Brenton, Howard Barker, Heathcote Williams, and David Edgar (see Chapter 9) who, in the late sixties and early seventies were writing specifically for small-scale theatres like The Theatre Upstairs and whose work usually demanded some form of environmental staging.

The Theatre Upstairs was in effect the first in a line of studio theatres which were to spring up in the seventies in direct response to the new work of both groups and playwrights. Most of these studio theatres were attached to the larger regional theatres, and they were always wide open to the accusation that they exploited the best of the work coming out of the fringe without, as Oval House had done, acting as a catalyst for its creation.

In the case of The Theatre Upstairs it is true that a number of playwrights whose work was produced there had already had earlier plays mounted in smaller, more impoverished fringe theatres or, like Howard Brenton, by a touring company like Portable Theatre. This is not to devalue the importance of The Theatre Upstairs but simply to define it more accurately in the context of the early history of the fringe. The commitment of Gaskill and Wright to the new playwrights was at least expressed in a concrete, tangible form, and at a time when practical help was badly needed. Their decision to segregate the work in a studio theatre was made partly on economic grounds – they were convinced that it would not draw large enough audiences in the main auditorium at the Court – but was also justifiable for artistic reasons. Most of the shows that went into The Theatre Upstairs would not necessarily have benefited from being performed on a proscenium stage.

Set against this, however, are two further considerations. During the late seventies there were at least two productions – Thomas Babe's *A Prayer for My Daughter* and Nigel Williams' *Class Enemy* – which successfully made the transition from The Theatre Upstairs to the Court's main stage. And Barrie Keeffe's *Sus*, which started life in a very small theatre (the Soho Poly), and was then seen at The Theatre Upstairs, subsequently did very well on the proscenium stage at The Theatre Royal, Stratford. It could be argued that none of these plays *needed* flexible, environmental staging. Indeed Max Stafford-Clark, the current artistic director at the Royal Court, now suspects that the previously accepted definition of an 'upstairs play' as opposed to a 'downstairs play' has been too narrow and restrictive. The fact remains that a 400-seat theatre is a rigorous test of the extent of public support for new work. A production drawing audiences of 100 or 150, which would pack out the Bush Theatre, would have to be accounted a box-office failure downstairs at the Royal Court.

The Bush.   The Bush Theatre, a small independent theatre in a room above a pub in Shepherd's Bush, has contributed consistently towards the growth and consolidation of the fringe since it opened in 1972. For the first year or more it could be said that the Bush succeeded almost despite itself, in that the programming was a very odd mixture indeed: some productions – an adaptation, for example, of John Fowles' best-selling novel *The Collector* – seemed to have been tailor-made for a prospective West End transfer, while at the opposite extreme visiting companies included 7:84 with their production of John Arden and Margaretta D'Arcy's *The Ballygombeen Bequest*.

By the mid-seventies Howard Gibbins and Peter Wilson, who had taken over the running of The Bush, had begun a policy of encouraging new British playwrights, a policy which has been refined and developed by

Foco Novo's production of *Independence* by Mustapha Matura at The Bush Theatre (1979) – a Chekhovian analysis of colonialist attitudes.

Dusty Hughes since he became artistic director in 1976. The first successes in this area – most notably the productions of Stephen Poliakoff's *Hitting Town* and *City Sugar* – were mostly plays by writers who had already established some kind of reputation. More recently, however, the principle of commissioning and producing first plays from non-established writers has borne real fruit with the critical and box-office success of Jonathan Gems' *The Tax Exile* and Julia Kearsley's *Wednesday*. (Gems, however, had had two short plays presented at lunchtime theatres.)

The list of playwrights whom one associates in some way with The Bush is impressive – Poliakoff, Snoo Wilson, Edgar, Robert Holman. But, despite a fair-sized Arts Council grant (by fringe standards) of £58,000 in 1979–80, economics still dictate that The Bush can afford to mount only six or seven of its own productions each year. Given the management's belief that the programme should change roughly once a month (unlike, say, Hampstead Theatre, where successful productions will often be given an extended run of eight or ten weeks), the home-grown productions have to be interspersed with plays from visiting companies, with which The Bush has often sought to build up a continuing relationship. Regular visitors have included Hull Truck and Foco Novo.

The performance space at The Bush is not perhaps quite as flexible as in some other theatres of the same size. Although in the past it has been used with a traverse stage, the basic arrangement now seems to be a rectangular performance area with two blocks of seating in an L-shape along two of the walls of the room. All this proves is that purely physical conditions, and the precise nature of a performance space, are not finally the most crucial factor in a theatre's success. The first requirement, as The Bush demonstrates, is a clear-cut and considered artistic policy. Eight years after The Bush opened, and twelve years after the first burgeoning of the fringe, Dusty Hughes describes his overall aims in the following terms: "I believe that you can't remain constantly a fringe theatre. Everyone's ambition should be to make fringe theatre the mainstream theatre, in the sense of making what was unorthodox a couple of years ago what everyone wants to see today." As evidence that this is possible, at least seven plays originally staged at The Bush have subsequently been shown on television – a clear indication that successful fringe plays are also accessible popular theatre.

The ICA Theatre.   Much the same impulse – that is, a concern to make fringe theatre more widely accepted and appreciated – is detectable in the current policy at the ICA Theatre in the Mall. Historically this theatre has played only a peripheral role in supporting the work of the fringe. Over recent years, however, and certainly since John Ashford arrived as director in April 1978, a more clear-cut strategy has been worked out and for the first time the theatre possesses a distinct identity.

The basic pattern of programming at the ICA is a familiar one: in 1979 Ashford could afford to produce only two of his own shows; for the remainder of the season other companies were brought in. Most of the visiting companies are established fringe heavyweights, for two reasons. Ashford is "... keen to prove that there is work around from the small-scale touring area which will fill 200 seats all the year round". (So, crudely, he cannot take too many chances on unfamiliar names.) He also wants to encourage established companies like The People Show "... to use this large performance space in an inventive way, to present the kind of show that they wouldn't be able to do anywhere else." His theatre's identity, he believes, must derive from the nature of the performance space itself, and from the distinctive uses to which it is put.

Ashford's policy with regard to playwrights is necessarily a limited one: the two ICA productions in 1979 were of plays by Snoo Wilson and

Shared Experience at the ICA with *Science Fictions* (1978), directed by Mike Alfred.

Stephen Poliakoff, both well established writers. "We simply can't afford to take risks on new writers. The only consolation I can offer them – and myself – is that in London perhaps the Bush, Hampstead Theatre, The Theatre Upstairs, and The Warehouse are sufficient provision for finding and putting on work by new playwrights."

Hampstead Theatre.   Mention of Hampstead Theatre and The Warehouse highlights the problems of erecting any secure and watertight definition of what constitutes a 'fringe' theatre. Hampstead Theatre is relatively small, independent, geographically non-West End, and has put on a great many new plays. The *type* of play to be seen there, however, is in general not very different from what one might expect from a regional repertory theatre; the shows are designed for a mainstream, middle-class audience, and quite a number of them have transferred to the West End. Hampstead has done little or nothing to sustain either the groups or the playwrights who have emerged from the fringe.

The King's Head.   Compare Hampstead Theatre with the even trickier case of the King's Head Theatre, Islington. *Physically* there can be no doubt that the King's Head fits the bill: a smallish room at the back of a pub, seating about 100, founded in 1970 by a Canadian, Dan Crawford, who also holds the licence to the pub. Crawford began in 1970 with evening shows, then introduced lunchtime theatre the following year. The King's Head is now probably one of the best-known fringe venues in London. But Crawford admits that he has "... never been particularly keen on the work of the performance groups" (although several of the groups have appeared there, particularly in the early 'seventies). He also agrees that the shows which best characterize the general policy at the King's Head have been plays like Robert Patrick's *Kennedy's Children* and Hugh Leonard's *Da*: the former transferred to the West End and ran there for nine months, while *Da* was next seen (in an American production) on Broadway. The King's Head has pioneered a form of downmarket cabaret theatre (patrons are given the opportunity of dining while they watch the play) and it has survived and thrived on the shrewd basis of small-scale productions which appeal to mainstream audiences.

The Open Space.   The Open Space Theatre, under Charles Marowitz, has followed a more experimental line, but it has not been one calculated to give aid and comfort to writers or touring groups. Marowitz's intention has always been to create a permanent company of actors and to develop an ensemble approach towards existing dramatic material – whether modern and avant-garde classics or his own collage versions of Shakespeare plays. It was never any part of his aims to serve as a base for new writers. Problems with funding (Marowitz is a highly articulate critic of Arts Council policies with regard to subsidies) ironically created a situation where, in order to survive in the original premises in a basement on Tottenham Court Road, he was forced into putting on a batch of relatively commercial new plays ". . . with an eye to transferring them into the West End, getting our name on the map, and attracting subsidy." This kind of disjunction between the stated aims of the Open Space and the oddly inconsistent programmes continued, if anything more acutely, when the theatre moved into a disused post-office on the Euston Road in 1977 and up to the closure of the theatre in 1979.

There is still one other category of small theatre which has appeared in the second half of the seventies – the studio theatres attached to the two giants, the RSC and the National Theatre. Even the briefest consideration of their position and function serves to highlight the importance of theatres like the ICA and Oval House maintaining their commitment towards forms of performance art and group-created theatre. Their establishment is also a measure of the influence the fringe has had on mainstream theatre.

The Other Place.   Neither of the RSC's studio theatres house productions originating from outside the Company. The Other Place in Stratford-upon-Avon was the brainchild of Buzz Goodbody, who ran it for a short while until her death in 1975. Under her strong leadership, activities in the first year had a clear educational and community orientation. A production of *Lear*, which had evolved in conjunction with discussions with local teachers, was taken out to schools, as was David Holman's touring show *The World Turned Upside Down*. Since then this side of the work has been largely dropped. The repertoire, which consists of Shakespeare, Jacobean plays, modern classics, and occasional new plays, is consciously designed to test a classical company in a small space which challenges techniques and habits developed for proscenium theatre.

The Warehouse.   The Warehouse, in Covent Garden, which opened in 1977, fits more precisely what one expects of a fringe theatre. Its bold policy of commissioning new work (from both new and established writers) and its practice of working closely with writers at all points, from the development of the initial idea for a play through to the finished script, is a valuable addition to the similar work carried out by The Bush and the Royal Court. Not only does the existence of The Warehouse increase the chances of a new writer getting a first production, it also extends the range and type of spaces which established playwrights can write for. One striking feature of the past few years is the mobility of playwrights like Poliakoff, Wilson, or Edgar who over a two or three year period might well have their plays produced at the Royal Court, The Bush, the ICA, and The Warehouse in turn.

The Cottesloe.   The Cottesloe, the smallest (although it seats 400!) and most flexible of the three theatres at the National, opened with *Illuminatus!*, a 7-hour long epic by Ken Campbell's Science Fiction Theatre of Liverpool. Despite this, and a number of visiting companies such as

Berkoff's London Theatre Group, the pattern of the programming firmly indicates that the main aim is to develop a more or less permanent company of actors and to extend the experiments in staging that Bill Bryden began with his 'promenade' productions of *The Passion* and *Lark Rise*. New plays may well form a part of the repertoire but it is clear that neither new writers nor visiting companies are foremost in Bryden's thoughts.

The National Theatre, like many other managements, will always pay lipservice to the idea of presenting new work. The real test is not so much the number of new plays produced, as the readiness of a theatre to back promising new writers, or performance groups, at a time when that commitment will count for something – before they have achieved any degree of prominence. Anything else smacks of exploitation or of an easy policy of backing those who are already identifiable as 'winners'.

Since the late sixties the main support for new work has come from the smaller 'fringe' theatres. This is not necessarily because the work was bound to draw small audiences, as Dusty Hughes at the Bush and John Ashford at the ICA are now demonstrating. It is because the small theatres possessed artistic directors and managements with the courage and conviction to take the necessary risks.

Their example might well serve as a model for *all* theatres in the eighties. When the Birmingham Arts Lab was born in 1968, like many others of its kind it lacked any permanent home. In its first premises, theatre events took place in one of two rooms, neither of them technically equipped as a theatre. Since it moved buildings in 1977 the position is even worse: economic cutbacks have meant that there is no immediate hope of fitting out a regular performance space. Despite this the Birmingham Arts Lab has been one of the more important venues for new work over the past ten years. It has served as the base for a dance company (the Birmingham Performance Group) and for a Writers' Theatre Company. And it has been responsible, together with the Chapter Arts Centre in Cardiff, for pioneering the idea of residencies for companies such as Welfare State, IOU, Pip Simmons, and Lumiere and Son.

The strength of any theatre lies not in its financial and physical resources, but in an imaginative and creative artistic policy.

References

1 *Time Out* No. 7, 16 December 1968–12 January 1969.
2 All quotes from individuals are from interviews with the author.

12 First Tragedy . . . Then Farce

The regional reps

Robin Thornber

Once upon a time the regional repertory theatres *were* the fringe. Now they are the mainstream of British theatre. Soon, when Shaftesbury Avenue withers away, they will be the establishment rearguard. Real drama is going on the streets, returning to the tradition of the strolling players from whence it came.

The Repertory Movement

Commercial theatre at the beginning of the century was popular, thriving, and profitable but it was more concerned with escapist entertainment than with 'high art', intellectual standards, or social relevance. In the provinces particularly, audiences were offered a dismal choice between pre-West End touring shows (publicly rehearsed try-outs), post-West End tours (pale imitations without the star names), or vaudeville. In response to this, the impulse behind what became known as the 'repertory movement' came from three sources. Firstly, there were audiences (or potential audiences) who wanted to see decent productions of the classics other than as set-piece snatches of Shakespeare or *Swan Lake* tucked into a pantomime programme; secondly, there were audiences – largely the self-educated, self-improving, self-conscious working people – who wanted to see contemporary, committed writing about the world they lived in; and thirdly, there were the artists themselves, or at least that small element of the theatrical profession – those actors, writers and directors who weren't totally caught up in the pyramid career structure that had regional touring and seaside follies at its base and Shaftesbury Avenue stardom at its apex. They wanted not only more interesting parts and less embarrassing lines to say, but an altogether different structure for the theatrical system.

Though the development of the repertory movement took place a long time ago, it was far more significant, indeed revolutionary, than the theatrical watershed of 1956. *Look Back in Anger* and the kitchen sink drama that followed were no more than a change of emphasis in content. The angry young men of the fifties and sixties wrote about unmarried mothers with underclothes steaming on the stove in a bedsitter instead of elegant lords and ladies at endless weekend house-parties. But they still wrote well-made plays and aimed them at the West End. What are *Look Back in Anger*, or *Roots*, but conventional love stories? But the 'grocers' theatres' at the beginning of the twentieth century actually changed the world – the little world of theatre at least – and set the pattern for the next two generations. They got the name, significantly, from the source of their funding, the private patrons whose inherited wealth derived from the bountiful breakfast tables of Edwardian England.

Annie Horniman, the tea heiress, started the repertory 'movement'. After establishing Ireland's national theatre at the Abbey in Dublin, she came to Manchester in 1908 and turned the Gaiety Theatre into a focal point for new writers (much as George Devine did with the Royal Court in the fifties). She had already championed Shaw in London and Yeats in Dublin. (This was at a time when dramatists like Shaw, Ibsen and Chekhov were considered so avant-garde that they were staged by private subscribers-only societies to evade the censorship of the Lord Chamberlain.) Of the 200 or so productions that Annie Horniman staged at the Gaiety during her first ten years in Manchester, over half were of new plays. Following John Galsworthy's *Justice* in 1910, a new group of writers emerged – the Manchester school. With comedies and dramas like Harold Brighouse's *Hobson's Choice* and Stanley Houghton's *Hindle Wakes*, these new writers depicted the reality of the time and place in which they lived.

One of Miss Horniman's protégés, Basil Dean, moved down the road to Liverpool in 1911 to turn the Star music hall into what is now the country's oldest surviving repertory theatre – the Liverpool Playhouse. And in Birmingham Sir Barry Jackson, whose wealth came from the Maypole grocery chain, found a home for his pre-war Pilgrim Players in the Birmingham Rep in 1913. Jackson, too, was a champion of Shaw (he started the Malvern Festival in 1929) and he also tried to liven up the classics by pioneering modern-dress Shakespeare. By 1932 he was running five separate repertory companies.

However, the early repertory movement was not just based on new, committed writing and an intelligent approach to the classics. It also prided itself on a local identity, on short runs and a changing programme, and on a resident ensemble company with no stars. But to achieve 'recognition' from audiences and within the profession the reps found themselves succumbing to the values of the West End – aiming at the accolade of London transfers or mimicking London successes. Barry Jackson actually bought two London theatres to provide his company with a metropolitan showcase.

Because of this all-pervasive, pernicious influence of Shaftesbury Avenue, the 'movement' which had begun as the dissenting fringe, the alternative theatre of the Edwardian stage, degenerated in the inter-war period into the appalling routine of tatty weekly rep, with in-experienced young hopefuls and weary, failed old troupers going through the inexorable motions of learning one script while rehearsing another and performing yet another. This history, though distant in time, is immediately, urgently relevant because what happened to the early, pioneering repertory movement is happening all over again to the second generation of subsidized civic reps.

The Second Wave

There were other factors which led to the decline of the repertory movement; but after the war, with the decline of the commercial touring circuits as the managements who had milked them in their heyday diverted their investment into new leisure markets like bingo, there came the second great resurgence of repertory. In some ways the reasons for this were similar – intelligent audiences felt neglected, actors wanted steady jobs with satisfactory parts. But this time there was a difference. The funding came not from wealthy private backers indulging in cultural evangelism as a hobby but from the Arts Council and the municipal authorities.

The first of the new reps was the Coventry Belgrade, built in 1958, which imported from Germany the civilized notion of the subsidized civic playhouse. This was quickly followed by other local authorities who

Annie Horniman, the doyenne of the Repertory Movement, established a thriving company at the Gaiety Theatre, Manchester, in 1908. A member of that company in its early days was Basil Dean, who became the first director of the Liverpool Repertory Theatre in 1911.

wished to demonstrate their sophistication and enlightenment in a competitive display of municipal culture palaces. After the Chichester Festival Theatre in 1962 came the Nottingham Playhouse (built from the windfall profit from selling off the gasworks); the Yvonne Arnaud at Guildford (1965); the Bolton Octagon (1967); the Chester Gateway (1968); and Leeds Playhouse (1970). Then came the wave of culture complexes like the Croydon Ashcroft, Billingham Forum and Wythenshawe Forum, and the new university campus theatres at Exeter, Sussex (Brighton), Stirling, Lancaster and Bradford.

A point to remember about the new wave of civic reps is that, being subsidized from the public purse and therefore bureaucratically accountable, they are all building-based rather than company-based. (The one possible exception is Stephen Joseph's company set up at Stoke-on-Trent in 1962. Although council-financed in its converted cinema, it retains, under Peter Cheeseman, the atmosphere of an old actor-manager's company.) This shift of emphasis becomes even more obvious with the further wave of local authority and Arts Council theatre building in the early seventies. These new playhouses were designed to replace and improve on existing, smaller repertory theatres and to rehouse their companies.

Newcastle upon Tyne's Playhouse was given to the amateurs in 1970 when the company moved into the new University Theatre; and at Sheffield, where the Playhouse dated from a first-generation rep formed by Herbert Prentice in 1923, the company moved into the new Crucible in 1971, the same year that Birmingham Rep got its new glass and concrete home. In 1973 Robin Midgley's company moved from the Phoenix, Leicester's tentative rep built ten years earlier, into the smart new Haymarket, part of a civic shopping precinct. And a similar development occurred in Manchester, where the then Theatre 69 left the University Theatre on its way to settling in the Royal Exchange. Both in Leicester and in Manchester the vacated buildings came to house a new, specialist young people's theatre company.

The Nottingham Playhouse presented *Brassneck* by David Hare and Howard Brenton in 1974. Although it was later adapted for television, the play has never been seen on the London stage.

It is obviously a romantic myth, and a sort of inverted snobbery, to say that exciting drama can only come out of converted church halls or the upper rooms of public houses, or that good work is impossible with the technically sophisticated facilities of modern civic playhouses. But there are inevitably sobering effects which flow from being responsible on the one hand to a board of local worthies and on the other to the Arts Council (who won't necessarily share the same approach) as well as feeling obliged to fill a large auditorium. Many of the new civic reps are as big as (or often bigger than) many West End theatres while at the same time having a smaller catchment area, a less well-established theatre-going tradition, and little or no tourist trade. (In particular, the new civic playhouses – e.g. at Sheffield, Birmingham, Leicester, Derby – often doubled the capacity, and the maintenance costs, of the old repertory theatres they replaced.) However, the increasing pressure on theatre directors and administrators (a significant new role) to fill every seat comes not just from economic causes, although that is vitally important. There is, too, a moral obligation. If the theatre derives part of its income from the ratepayers – and probably through an unsympathetic but crucial committee of philistine councillors – it dare not appear to be catering exclusively for an elitist, arty-crafty minority.

For these reasons and in order to justify their subsidy, the shiny new playhouses of the sixties, monuments to civic pride and planners' dreams, had to set out in search of an audience. This also suited the new wave of directors, writers, and many of the performers, who emerged as the job opportunities opened up. This new generation, in reaction against the previous generation's tradition of star-struck, camp theatricality (the Donald Wolfit school of roundly enunciating actors with the stress on the final syllable) were, typically, grammar school and redbrick university-educated with well-preserved regional accents. They were into de-mystifying the theatre, escaping from the spurious glamour of the plush and gilt pros arch and the star system. There was to be no fake illusion: lighting grids were put on display. Similarly, actors were technicians, not magicians; acting was a job, just the same as plumbing. Often the ideas came from Brecht but the accompanying revolution was invariably only a revolution in style not reality, the new rep theatre workers affecting being unaffected.

Nevertheless there was an idealism in the sixties, a belief that theatre had things to say and satisfactions to offer to a wider public than was traditionally assumed. This – or the way we went about it – may have been naive, but it was far more healthy than what had gone before – Coward and Rattigan, dressing for dinner and carriages at eleven. So the search for a new, wider and more popular audience in the repertory theatres of the sixties (or at least some of them) led once again to a change of content as well as style. While the Home Counties and more rural reps continued faithfully to ape the fifties' West End tradition of glamorous star-studded thrillers and sexploitation farces, those in the industrial towns of the North and Midlands began to look again at the world around them.

In some cases the very existence of a local repertory theatre, closely and *naturally* rooted in its community, can stimulate the development of new writing talent. But this is rare. Bill Naughton owes nothing to Bolton Octagon, nor Henry Livings to Oldham Coliseum, although eventually their plays may be staged there. More often it's the other way round. A writer who has made himself a national reputation but chosen to live in the provinces can find himself virtually carrying his local theatre – like Alan Ayckbourn at Scarborough or Alan Plater in Hull.

Television, with its bigger buying power and prestige, can sometimes do it. Granada's Manchester studios provided patronage for a whole new school of northern writing from *Z-Cars* on. But the Tyneside writers assembled for the first series of *When the Boat Comes In* were spotted not by Tyne-Tees Television but by the BBC's London-based producers. However, sometimes it can happen. Peter Cheeseman's Victoria Theatre-in-the-round in Stoke-on-Trent has wooed a local audience with local material – "celebrating the local community"[1] as he calls it – since 1962. The one truly indigenous writer that the process has produced, Arthur Berry, is not the most outstanding: competent, in a homely, local way, but no world-beater.

Cheeseman's success – and it was his achievement as a uniquely gifted, if quirkily autocratic, director – attracted a talented and committed company of performers and writers to live and work in Stoke, including Peter Terson, Ken Campbell, Chris Bond, Bob Eaton, Nick Darke and Tony Perrin. At its worst this approach can degenerate into a sort of local name-dropping of the kind you get in panto. But it can also produce some surprisingly good material. Stoke once staged a perfectly jolly musical called *Hands Up! For You the War is Ended*, based on the wartime memories of the newsagent across the road from the theatre. And at its best it soars. Their adaptation of Bennett's *Anna of the Five Towns* became a BBC costume classic and their musical documentary *The Knotty*, about the building of the North Staffordshire railway, went down a bomb in Italy. As Cheeseman says, the more intensely localized and specific you are, the more universal the truths you reveal.[2]

Another theatre which developed its own style and found its own talent, this time from its own local community, is the Liverpool Everyman. Set up in 1964 specifically as a young people's theatre in an old Methodist chapel by Peter James and Terry Hands, it rang bells with a particular section of the city's vital, cosmopolitan, bolshy community: the students, poets, lecturers, trade unionists, drunks and Scouse bohemia of Liverpool 8. Like Stoke they like musicals in Liverpool. But where the Vic's music tends to derive through folk harmonies from Methodist hymnody, the Everyman's music is heavy rock. The Everyman audiences also like local history, particularly if it documents a recent working-class struggle, such as Chris Bond's *Under New Management*, about the take-over by a workers' cooperative at Kirkby's Fisher-Bendix factory. For me, however, their most successful show was an affectionate biography of Bessie Braddock, the Labour politician who came as near as anyone ever has to running Liverpool. Their most famous production was *John, Paul, Ringo, George . . . and Bert*, the documentary about the Beatles by Willy Russell, which transferred successfully to London's West End.

Alan Dossor's regime as artistic director at the Everyman attracted writers like John McGrath and Ted Whitehead, and they in turn attracted

Above: Peter Cheeseman, director of the Victoria Theatre, Stoke, interviewing workers at the steelworks for the play *Fight for Shelton Bar* (1974) and *right:* rehearsing for *Jowl, Jowl and Listen Lads!* the pit safety variety show created by local coal-miners (1977).

audiences of working-class youngsters, some of whom had gone into teaching and later turned out to be writers like Willy Russell and Alan Bleasdale, because the Everyman had opened their minds to what theatre can do. At one time Dossor seemed to be developing a Liverpool school, taking in writers like Bill Morrison and Mike Stott, who were mining a rich vein of rude comedy among the mid-life suburbanites.

But the point about new writing, of the worthwhile rather than the worthy sort, is that it can't be contrived or even coaxed; it just seems to happen when the chemistry works between a director and the writers he or she stumbles across. The local documentary compiled by a resident writer has worked with audiences in other places – for Alan Cullen with *The Stirrings in Sheffield on a Saturday Night*, and for Rony Robinson just about everywhere he goes – but on the whole it doesn't often throw up major new talent.

Then there was the craze for rock musicals, following the success of *Jesus Christ, Superstar!: Joseph and His Amazing Technicoloured Dreamcoat*, and *Godspell*. At least it got theatre directors involved with their local rock bands but none of the results I saw was totally successful, either artistically or at the box office.

Essays into openly political theatre are rare among the repertory companies themselves, although they will occasionally bring in touring companies with a socialist bias, such as 7:84 or Belt & Braces. The exceptions, of course, are those where the theatre board has leftish leanings – like the Everyman – or, like the Library Theatre in Manchester, where a well-established director, David Scase, is answerable to a traditionally Labour-controlled council. But these self-conscious attempts to widen the appeal of repertory programming have not met with much success in changing the social composition of audiences, who tend to remain as conservative, lower middle-class, middle-aged, middle-brow, and West End-orientated as ever.

The exception to this rule has been the Citizens Theatre in Glasgow. Situated in the Gorbals, and directed for ten years by Giles Havergal, the Citizens has, almost uniquely amongst repertory theatres, developed its own individual style. This is solidly based in the 'art' theatre tradition and has little truck with the more obviously community-orientated theatrical genres. (However, just as importantly, the Citizens is situated in the heart of its locality and not set apart from it; its ambiance is informal and welcoming and, as a cornerstone of its policy, it keeps its seat prices very low.) With his designer, Philip Prowse, and his dramaturg, Robert David MacDonald – the Citizens genuinely work as a team – Havergal has developed a form of theatre which relies for its effect as much on visuals as on writing. Design and visual flair goes hand in hand with a resolute anti-naturalism and an attachment to the theatrical. It is also allied with a desire to shock – or, at least, an ability to be frequently immersed in controversy. The audiences at the Citizens which, incidentally was established in 1943, cannot be classified as working class. But, by making experiment the central value of their work and by sticking to their guns, the Citizens has cultivated an audience which is free-thinking, non-parochial, receptive to different theatrical forms and passionately disputatious.

Studio Theatres

The solution for many of the newer reps has been to split their audiences into two: with a main auditorium, seating 700–800 and having a fairly middle-of-the-road policy, and a 100–200-seat studio with a more adventurous, experimental programme.

This can work both ways. Certainly much of the most interesting and exciting work in the past few years has been found in the studios. Their smaller capacity allows directors to try out new work by writers whose names are not well enough known to draw a main house audience. And they are, on the whole, designed and built in such a way as to allow a more flexible approach to patterns of staging, with movable seats and a full lighting grid. One splendid example of this was at the Sheffield Crucible, where studio director David Leland was given his own company for two solid seasons devoted entirely to new work. It enabled him to stage Dennis Potter's banned television play *Brimstone and Treacle*, for instance, and to draw attention to new writers like Ron Hutchinson and Victoria Wood as well as giving a first airing to works of more established writers, such as Howard Barker's *The Love of a Good Man*.

Another intelligent use of the studio came with William Gaunt's tenure of the Liverpool Playhouse towards the end of the seventies. A studio programme which included stunning productions of Nigel Williams' *Class Enemy*, Barry Collins' *Judgement*, and Barrie Keeffe's *Sus* (a programme which would once have looked more at home in the Everyman) didn't prevent him from staging David Hare's *Plenty* in the main auditorium.

Studios give a director a much wider range of options in the setting of a play, adjusting from open end, thrust, traverse, or in-the-round staging, depending on the nature of the work. Birmingham's Brum Rep studio, for instance, used a traverse set to brilliant effect to recreate the shop floor of a small engineering works for Stephen Bill's *The Old Order*.

Studios also have the advantage of being available for use by smaller scale companies – either in-house teams like community touring or theatre-in-education groups, or bought-in small-scale touring companies like Paines Plough or Foco Novo. And this is one point where even the more conservative, staid repertory companies can come in with the more exciting experiments which are going on outside the mainstream of conventional drama. In the early seventies, for instance, there was a great

deal of creative energy being released in and around west Yorkshire, based
on a nexus between Albert Hunt, Jeff Nuttall, and John and Sue Fox's
Welfare State. Because of the way they worked – mainly in the streets –
they had little impact on Leeds Playhouse's main programme. Most
theatre-goers would hardly have been aware of their existence. It was
Roger Chapman's theatre-in-education team that involved them in an
international children's theatre festival, based on the Playhouse.

This is one of the ironies of the way that the reps have been developing
in the past few years – that the most interesting, the most promising
activities, have been taking place not in the main auditorium but in the
studio or with loosely attached community and theatre-in-education
teams based on the studio or even working outside the theatre altogether.
The precursor of this was Ken Campbell, who developed his original
roadshow for community tours of pubs and clubs first from the Stoke
Victoria and then from the Bolton Octagon.

The main argument against having a theatre studio in the first place has
always been that it provides a safety valve, a cop-out for the director's
artistic conscience that allows him to play safe in the main auditorium.
Theatres without a studio are compelled, to keep their self-respect, to be
more adventurous in their main house policy. It is perhaps significant that
those reps with the most enterprising programmes (in terms of new work)
in their main auditoria are the ones without a studio – Stoke Victoria,
Liverpool Everyman, Nottingham Playhouse, Glasgow Citizens. And the
converse of this is true. When a theatre has a studio which is doing lively
and original work – like Birmingham's Brum Rep staging David Edgar and
Stephen Bill in the late seventies, its main house programme becomes
more middle of the road, with thoroughly glossy, star-studded revivals of,
say, John Gay's *Beggars' Opera*.

This became a worrying trend after the repertory bubble burst with the
local authority spending cuts in the mid-seventies. Faced with costs that

Patti Love as *Mary Barnes*.
David Edgar's play,
adapted from an
autobiographical account
of a "journey through
madness", was premiered
at the Birmingham Rep
Studio Theatre in 1978.

were escalating faster than the retail price index, and the freezing of subsidy, which meant a drop in real income, theatre managements were increasingly forced to keep a wary eye on their box office revenue – and that means playing safe. So, whereas even the second-generation reps had been created in response to a demand for a more intelligent alternative to the trash the declining commercial theatre had to offer, with the final demise of the commercial touring circuits the subsidized theatre was edged over to take its mainstream, middle-of-the-road place.

At one time only a handful of smart, southern repertory theatres would aim at West End transfers – Bristol, Guildford, Chichester. The effect of the subsidy straitjacket is that more and more are aiming at this sort of 'success'.

There have been some strange examples of the way this mixed economy approach has developed, with commercial managements using set-building and rehearsal facilities of subsidized civic theatres. For example, at Billingham Forum, Les Jobson, lacking a resident company of his own, signed a series of co-production deals with commercial managements who opened their shows there, and then toured in hope of a West End opening. Right back to the pre-war set-up, but with public subsidy mixed up with private speculation. The mixed economy has developed still further at Birmingham Rep, where the process is two-way. Successful Rep productions are sold to commercial managements to prolong their life and recoup costs. And artistic director Clive Perry economizes by buying in commercial packages. The ultimate development of this was in the Arts Council's co-productions with Cameron Mackintosh of the musicals, *My Fair Lady* and *Oklahoma!*, for regional touring, with an eye on West End transfers.

Other regional repertory theatres have been pooling resources and sharing costs with co-productions, e.g. the joint Nottingham Playhouse/ Sheffield Crucible version of *Hotel Paradiso*. This sort of spreading of production costs and extending the life of a production can make sense in some circumstances. Theatre Clwyd at Mold, for instance, sends some of its productions around the splendid touring circuit in Wales. Tyneside Theatre Company was set up specifically to operate in several theatres in the northeast. But the selection of programmes and the building of productions with a canny eye on the possibility of a West End transfer can only, in the long run, have an unsettling effect on repertory theatres' policies. It can only result in a return to the pre-war situation where repertory was regarded as a training ground for London. And in the end that can only be unhealthy for the rest of the country.

References

1 Peter Cheeseman in an interview with the author.
2 *ibid.*

"Incongruity attracts attention": demonstration outside Bow Street Magistrates Court in 1978 protesting against the harassment of street entertainers. One group, Demolition Decorators, were prosecuted 23 times in London in 1978–79. There were only two convictions, the rest being acquittals or discharges.

13 The Bitten Hand

Patronage and alternative theatre

Sandy Craig

In 1969/70 Arts Council subsidy to alternative theatre was £15,000. In 1978/79, from the Drama Panel of the Arts Council alone, it was over £1.5 million. The total public subsidy in that year was in excess of £2 million. From about a dozen part-time companies living off the dole and meagre box-office takings in 1968, there are now around sixty full-time companies subsidized by the Arts Council plus a similar number of ad-hoc companies who present one or two shows each year. There are also some Regional Arts Association subsidized companies.

This is a staggering achievement: in a decade when material costs have risen four times, when average wages have risen about twenty times (in 1968 they were often only £3–4 per week) the groups have multiplied ten-fold and the subsidy increased over one thousand fold. Moreover, this has been achieved in the face of entrenched ideological opposition and bureaucratic mystification from within the Arts Council and apathy within Equity (the actors' union) and the other concerned trade unions. At the same time the alternative theatre companies have established a nationwide network of venues in which to present their work. Some of these are, of course, the studio theatres of the regional reps or established arts centres. But many are community, trade union and village halls, working men's clubs and other venues where before there was no theatre and where now theatre is only one activity among many.

The increased importance of alternative theatre is shown in yet another way. Ten years ago alternative theatre was hardly reviewed at all, except by *Time Out*. Nowadays new productions at the major fringe theatres in London and productions by the larger and better established touring companies are reviewed as a matter of course in the 'serious' daily and weekly papers. Yet despite this achievement there is a feeling within alternative theatre of anomie. Partly this can be explained in terms of the downturn of political activity and an increasingly philistine society. Partly it can be explained by the psychological cliche that the excitement engendered by the new cannot be sustained for long: dedication has to replace dilettantism. There is also the feeling that alternative theatre is perhaps no longer so different from mainstream theatre as it once was. And this explanation is backed up by the increasing numbers of actors, writers and other theatre workers who have 'graduated' from alternative theatre to the National and other prestigious companies. But this anomie can also be explained, firstly, by the fact that though subsidy has dramatically increased over the past ten years, it has hardly increased at all (in real terms) over the past five years, and secondly, by the relations of production, the system of finance and distribution, in which the work takes place. These are dominated by the Arts Council.

The Arts Council

The Arts Council was created in 1946 from CEMA (the Council for the Encouragement of Music and the Arts). This was one of the two war-time organizations set up by the government to boost morale, the other being ENSA, the Entertainments National Service Association. CEMA promoted the arts, ENSA entertainment. From opposite ends these organizations began to bridge the cultural divide which decreed that the arts were for the middle class and entertainment was for the working class. Just as the Welsh miners discovered the power of Sybil Thorndyke, so the middle classes came to enjoy the work of dance bands, singers and comedians. But, at the end of the war, ENSA fell by the wayside. While the Labour government tried to create the basis for a more egalitarian society, the 'culture gap' was reinstated.

The Arts Council's Royal Charter established its objects as "to develop and improve the knowledge, understanding and practice of the arts" and "to increase the accessibility of the arts to the public throughout Great Britain". Unlike CEMA, which had promoted amateur performance of music and theatre, the Arts Council restricted itself to subsidizing professional artists. Meanwhile, for twenty years, its policy was biased very much towards the first of its objectives. It saw its primary function in terms of raising the quality of the work of existing companies, a policy it commemorated in the slogan 'few but roses'. Only with the advent of a Labour government and its Arts Minister Jennie Lee in the mid-sixties did the Arts Council fully embrace both objectives. This move coincided with other developments in the arts, in particular the creation nationwide of new regional repertory theatres.

The Arts Council is a *quango* (quasi-autonomous national government organization). It is funded directly by the Ministry of Arts, whose Minister appoints the Arts Council's governing body, The Council, (made up of voluntary members) and its most senior, full-time official, the Secretary-General. The Council in turn appoints the voluntary members of panels and committees, who serve in their capacity as individuals and not as representatives of any artistic trade union or other organization. Within its grant from the government, the Arts Council exercises its own discretion about how the Treasury's money is to be distributed. In this sense the Arts Council is independent of government.

In turn the Arts Council sits at the apex of a three-tier system. Beneath the Arts Council are the twelve English Regional Arts Associations (RAAs) plus the Scottish and Welsh Arts Councils. Beneath the Regional Arts Associations are the local authorities. The RAAs receive the bulk of their money from the Arts Council, though they are also subsidized by the local authorities in their region (roughly an 80/20 split). The Regional Arts Associations are independent of the Arts Council though there is, of course, much pooling of information.

The overriding difficulty that the Arts Council has always faced is that it is the main body of *public* patronage in Britain. This difficulty has been recognized openly only fleetingly (during the mid-sixties and again in the mid-seventies) when plans were proposed for a pluralist form of arts

An Independent Theatre Council demonstration outside the Arts Council headquarters in 1979, protesting against the threatened closure of London's Action Space: the theatre was saved.

patronage with central and local government, private industry and the unions all playing major roles in subsidizing the creative artist. These plans, however, came to nothing. Meantime the Arts Council suffers alone the main problem of public patronage. This is that, whereas an individual can patronize whatever he likes and for whatever reason and cannot be challenged for his choice, a public authority has to claim that it is acting on behalf of the 'public' and that its choices are not dictated by individual bias or private whim.

The Arts Council has chosen a double strategy in an attempt to overcome this problem. Firstly, it argues that it is accountable only in purely financial terms. It cannot be artistically accountable because that would threaten its independence, an independence necessary for the preservation of the freedom of the artist. This in turn ensures the health of the arts. (Of course, the health of the arts is not necessarily dependent on the freedom of the artist: artists weren't conspicuously freer in Elizabethan England and yet that was the period of our finest dramatic flowering.) This fetishization of its 'independence' has resulted in the Arts Council being obsessively and paranoically anti-democratic. Thus panel members serve as individuals not as representatives of other organizations, while companies are not given any reason why they are subsidized or not.

The second strand of strategy is enshrouded in the Arts Council's ideology which accepts that it is accountable – but to a set of ideas, ideas about art, culture, civilization, standards and forms of behaviour. Its idea of art is as the embodiment of 'imaginative truth' – a delicate elixir bringing nobility, wisdom and spiritual balm to those fortunate enough to appreciate it. Its idea of civilization is derived from the ideas of critics like Leavis: civilization is guaranteed only by a strong tradition of art. (Adherents of this idea find themselves hard-pressed to explain the state-supported Nazi opera or the Stalinist-supported ballet.) Part of art's holy mission is to educate to an appreciation of art those unfortunates (normally identified as youth or the working class) who live philistine existences.

At one extreme this belief is expressed in terms of social engineering. Thus Lord Goodman, a former Chairman of the Arts Council, said in 1967:

> "I believe that there is a crucial state in the country at this moment. I believe that young people lack values, lack certainties, lack guidance; that they need something to turn to; and need it more desperately than they have needed it at any time in our history – certainly, at any time which I can recollect. I do not say that the arts will furnish a total solution . . . [but] I believe that once young people are *captured* for the arts they are *redeemed* from many of the dangers which are occupying the attention of the Government in a completely unprofitable and destructive fashion."[1]

Art both assuages social passions and provides a smoke-screen behind which the reality of capitalist exploitation can continue. This is obviously not the view of art espoused by the alternative theatre companies. Indeed, their view is often the opposite – that art is an agent of change, not a bulwark of tradition. Both the companies and the Arts Council recognize this radical difference of views. As Sir Roy Shaw, current Secretary-General of the Arts Council, states:

> "A recent writer in *The Stage*, defending the fact that much community theatre is left-wing, says it 'has had to live with the contradictions of "biting the hand that feeds", of working to overthrow the State that enables it to work at all'. It apparently did not occur to the writer that this paradox might be harder for the state and the Arts Council to live with than for community theatre workers. Lord Goodman, when Chairman of the Arts Council, questioned whether it was the duty of the state actually to subsidize those who are working to overthrow it. The question remains."[2]

Two things follow from the Arts Council's position as a quango. Because it is artistically accountable to no one, it must judge companies only on artistic merit. It cannot – and it must be seen not to – judge on political grounds. On the other hand, though it is aesthetically independent of government, it is totally dependent economically. This dependence is made more precarious precisely because it is outside government and Whitehall. It has no direct access to the levers of power. It must attempt to avoid large visible controversies. And it must take into account the mood of the government of the time.

This has led the Arts Council to adopt a varying combination of two contradictory stances to alternative theatre. The first embodies a refusal to subsidize through a combination of bureaucratic inertia and misrecognition of the nature of the activity. This was the stance of the late sixties and early seventies. It was a stance which was broken through only by the concerted effort of the groups in a campaign organised by the Independent Theatre Council (a body set up and composed of the companies) and aided from within by a radical and articulate New Activities Committee on the Drama Panel supported by a sympathetic Drama Director, Nicholas Barter.

The second stance attempts to incorporate these new, radical activities within the mainstream. Thus John Faulkner, current Drama Director, states:

> "For a decade or more it has been possible for the Council to help those who want to extend the limits of the formal manner, content or audience of drama. This has been the area in which comparatively small subsidies can help the continual need for renewal. These companies also have the potential for exciting greater public outcry than could have been expected of a supposedly minority interest. One

need however only to look back over the recent past to see how quickly what was initially regarded as experimental has been assimilated into the fabric of today's theatre. The aim for the future must be to maintain this integration and not to create more and more new categories."[3]

The Arts Council used to think that the standards of the alternative theatre failed to meet the professional standards of the subsidized bourgeois and the West End commercial theatre. Nowadays it does think that alternative theatre measures up. It has passed quality control. But the real question is: can alternative theatre be judged by the same set of standards as the National Theatre or St Martins? The Arts Council insists that there is only a single set of standards applicable to every form of theatre. It does not accept a pluralist view of artistic activities – the view that there are different forms of art each with their own distinctive rules, standards and functions. To accept this both focuses on the materiality of artistic practice and denies the harmonious unity of 'all great art'. As Shaw says,

"I don't believe that there are middle-class art forms, I believe that there are only art forms which because of our social and educational history have been available only to the middle class but which are potentially available to all people."[4]

The Pressures of Patronage
The most obvious effects of the contradiction between the groups and the Arts Council are the occasional acts of censorship. In December 1972, for instance, 7:84 Theatre Company decided, on legal advice, to withdraw *The Ballygombeen Bequest* by John Arden and Margaretta D'Arcy, at that time playing at the Bush Theatre. They had received a letter from a firm of solicitors, headed by Lord Goodman, who were acting for a Sussex estate agent and landlord. The Ardens were later taken to court and found guilty of libel. The action against 7:84 was, however, dropped. But the next year, instead of being funded on a yearly revenue grant – as they had expected – they were funded project by project. Again, four years later, after the furore caused by their production *The Nine Days and Saltley Gates*, Foco Novo were funded at a level less than had been expected and less than was justified by the group's touring successes. However, there is no proof of direct political censorship in either case. Instead, as Malcolm Griffiths, a member of the Drama Panel at the time, has noted, the examples of such cases ". . . indicates the way the Arts Council can use its internal structure directly to affect the work of a company it disapproves of by shunting it around inside itself."[5]

But, as already noted, the Arts Council wishes to steer clear of large visible controversies – one of which is censorship. In this it is different from certain of the Regional Arts Associations. For instance, in 1978, North West Arts attempted to cut its grant to a political touring company,

North West Spanner. This move was instituted by a group of Conservative Councillors on the Management Council of North West Arts. It was only defeated after a long battle, a battle won by a quickly organized grass roots campaign of art workers, trade unionists and local activists. This example throws into relief the difference in thinking between the Arts Council and the Regional Arts Associations. These latter, though generally they receive less than a quarter of their subsidy from the local authorities within their region, have much larger local government representation on their management committees. This is reflected not just in numbers but in the fact that those local councillors are there, not as individuals, but as local councillors and as representatives of their political party. Such people naturally see the arts in the context of the overall development of their locality. There is no divorce between art and life. And, whether from motives of self-publicity or from the genuine concern of the elected representative, they have no compunction to hide their views or actions from the public gaze. In the North West Spanner case the whole controversy was conducted out in the open, drawing in Sir Roy Shaw to make a statement emphasizing that companies should be judged purely on artistic criteria and not political ones.

There are, however, more important constraints on the groups than those imposed by overt censorship: the constraints imposed by inbred thinking and by policy decisions which are 'concealed in the interstices of administrative decisions'. Implicit in the Arts Council's thinking is a commitment to the form of subsidized theatre which mushroomed from the Royal Court 'revolution' of 1956. This is a form of subsidized theatre which demands a theatre building in which to present the work. The Arts Council's bias can be explained in financial terms: it would be wasteful after so much capital expenditure to let those buildings rot. But the bias can also be explained because of the type of theatre that is presented there (or at least the type of theatre that it is thought is presented there). Rep theatre, with its literary values, its production standards, and its attempts to attract 'a local audience' out in the sticks embodies the Arts Council's idea of dramatic art.

The Arts Council is biased not only towards the rep theatre. It is biased against the experimental. At the present moment an ingrowing conservatism allied to a desire not to cause controversy and a wish to appear equitable corresponds with a tendency to self-perpetuation within the reps. This tendency continues regardless of whether or not there is any social or aesthetic requirement from society for the companies to continue or any artistic impulse from within the companies.

Perhaps most importantly for alternative theatre companies, however, is the fact that the institutional practices of the Arts Council seek to impose a different way of working on them which, because of their financial dependence on the Arts Council, they find hard to resist. For instance, the

Arts Council recognizes the position of artistic director but shows little confidence in a cooperative collective as the controlling body of the company. Again it pressurizes companies into a form of productivity deal which requires them to perform so many times per year. This genteel and hidden persuasion is instituted through the practice of asking companies for estimates – and not only financial estimates but touring and performance plans.

The pattern of performance is further defined by the Arts Council in a long standing policy. Some years ago the Arts Council recognized that the dominant mode of production within alternative theatre was touring. To encourage this they instituted a number of schemes, some of them in partnership with the Regional Arts Associations. Extra money was set aside for companies who toured under these schemes. In one scheme groups were encouraged to perform in the studio theatres and arts centres. In another groups toured five one-night stands in a region. But in this scheme the Regional Arts Associations helped to set up the tours and to choose the venues, often from previous contacts in the local arts world. There is nothing particularly conspiratorial about this. Indeed Regional Arts Associations are keen that every locality within their region is served by theatre. Touring companies are needed to provide this service and, because of the lack of theatres in many parts of the country, these must be small-scale and adaptable. (Besides which, most Regional Arts Associations do not have large budgets.) However, all these policies help to define not only where the groups play but to whom they play. A Mass Observation survey commissioned by the Arts Council showed that, in general, the groups played to much the same middle-class audiences as the rep theatres – though the audiences were significantly younger. What the survey also showed was that in those venues organized by the groups as part of their policy specifically to play to a working-class audience, their audience was, in fact, working class. Thus at Clay Cross 67% of 7:84's audience was drawn from a manual worker background while at Workington the figure was 37%.[6] Venues and, to a lesser extent, presenting managements define their own audiences: the working class does not go to the new concrete subsidized reps.

Despite the fact that the presence of an audience is one of the few defining characteristics of all theatre, many commentators regard the question of who makes up that audience as unimportant and extrinsic to the play itself. This view presupposes a number of doubtful ideas: firstly, that all people are substantially the same; secondly, that the audience does not affect the course of the production on stage, in other words, that the direction of flow of meaning is one-way, from stage to audience; thirdly, that the meaning of the play is unproblematical and that the audience is composed of individual, passive spectators on whose minds, like wiped-clean slates, the meaning of the play is writ. Alternative theatre knows otherwise: audiences – and therefore venues – are crucial.

But the Arts Council's way of thinking invades the practice of alternative theatre in another, more diffuse, way. It sets up patterns of expectation. Thus, Roland Muldoon of CAST:

> "It's like self-censorship. We start saying: 'The Arts Council want big plays because by that we'll make more money and they'll give us more money, so we'll have to take big plays to the working class.' So we start spreading the whole thing and what we could have said in fifteen minutes, we take one hundred and fifteen minutes."[7]

Of course, the Arts Council is not monolithic. Nor is there a conscious conspiracy at work within the Arts Council to implement either a policy to axe alternative theatre or to incorporate it. And there are, of course, many gains in the present system. Certainly the groups were not passive spectators in this process of increasing subsidy. In fact this whole process would never have occurred without the substantial efforts of the Independent Theatre Council, The Association of Community Theatres and other organizations. The Arts Council only opened the door to subsidy because the groups were already banging on it. The touring schemes that were set up by the Arts Council and the Regional Arts Associations, were set up in response to the initiatives of the groups. Similarly the unionization of this area of theatre was the initiative of the groups, an initiative which forced the Arts Council to recognize that grants had to be based on minimum union-agreed wages. And the emergence of the Theatre Writers' Union has been instrumental in forcing the Arts Council to pay writers adequately. Besides, the dependency of the groups is by no means total. Many alternative theatre companies continue to use this system of subsidy for their own aims rather than those of the Arts Council.

Absolute freedom is illusory; constraints on action are not necessarily bad. They can be positive or negative. I have argued that the political and financial constraints of the late sixties and early seventies may have had

The shell of The Albany Empire in Deptford in the summer of 1978. Arson was suspected but not proven. The theatre was rebuilt and in operation again within a year.

positive creative effects, while the system of dependency on the Arts Council and its control of finance and distribution impose mainly negative constraints at the present time. And this is, perhaps, one of the main causes for the present anomie of many groups.

However, there is an inherent tendency in all history to objectify an on-going process and to seal the heterogeneous activities and material wills of many different people into the tomb not only of easy categorization but of the instant past. It is easy to suggest that what was once revolutionary is now imbued with a trade union, reformist consciousness. Similarly, histories of the 'fringe' written in 1973, in 1974 and in 1976 have all said that it was over, dying. Like the famous novel it is taking a long time over it.

As I write there are a number of hopeful trends and new departures: it is evident that the heirs to The People Show and Welfare State have at last arrived; that feminist and gay theatre are beginning to achieve a continuity of tradition; that political theatre has made a lasting impression; and that the shift to various forms of satiric cabaret is more than a passing fad. Meanwhile the fund-raising benefit for the Blair Peach Campaign in 1979 points not only to a new spirit of cooperation between companies but also resurrected the fine old tradition of effigy burning. If alternative theatre is seen as a phoenix – continually emerging, continually being threatened with incorporation into an impoverished mainstream – then it is not being overly optimistic to see it as rising again from those ashes.

References

1 Lord Goodman in the House of Lords, 19 April 1967, quoted in *The Arts Council of Great Britain*, Nicholas Pearson, *New Arts* No. 2, Early Summer 1979.

2 Sir Roy Shaw in his introduction to *Patronage and Responsibility* 34th Annual Report of the Arts Council of Great Britain, 1979. p. 9.

3 John Faulkner in *Patronage and Responsibility, op. cit.* p. 15.

4 Sir Roy Shaw in an interview in *Time out* No. 502, 30 November–6 December 1979.

5 I should add that sometimes the Arts Council is so overstretched that decisions are reached that can be accounted to personal bias: I speak from experience on the New Applications and Projects sub-committee of the Drama Panel.

6 Report of the Survey of Small-scale Drama Groups' Audiences (Mass Observation, July 1978).

7 Roland Muldoon in an interview in *The Leveller*, April 1978.

Select Bibliography

Alternative Theatre

Ansorge, Peter *Disrupting the Spectacle: Five Years of Experimental and Fringe Theatre in Britain* (Pitman, 1975)
Braden, Su *Artists and People* (Routledge & Kegan Paul, 1978)
Hunt, Albert *Hopes for Great Happenings: Alternatives in Education and Theatre* (Eyre Methuen, 1976)
Itzin, Catherine *Stages in the Revolution* (Eyre Methuen, 1980)
Moffat, Alistair *The Edinburgh Fringe* (Johnston & Bacon, 1978)
Nuttall, Jeff *Performance Art: Vol. 1 Memoirs, Vol. 2 Scripts* (John Calder, 1979)

General Background

Bentley, Eric (ed) *The Theory of the Modern Stage* (Penguin, rev. 1976)
Bradby, David, James, Louis, and Sharratt, Bernard (eds) *Performance and Politics in Popular Drama* (Cambridge, 1980)
Bradby, David and McCormick, John *People's Theatre* (Croom Helm, 1978)
Brockett, Oscar G. and Findlay, Robert R. *Century of Innovation, A History of European and American Theatre and Drama since 1870* (Prentice-Hall, N.J., 1973)
Craik, T. W. (ed) *The Revels History of Drama in English Vol. VII '1880 to the Present Day'* by Hugh Hunt, Kenneth Richards and John Russell Taylor (Methuen, 1978)
Elsom, John *Post-War British Theatre* (Routledge & Kegan Paul, 1976)
Enzensberger, Hans Magnus *Raids and Reconstructions* (Pluto, 1976)
Hayman, Ronald *British Theatre Since 1955* (Opus, 1979)
Hayman, Ronald *Theatre and Anti-theatre* (Secker and Warburg, 1979)
Roberts, Peter *Theatre in Britain* (Pitman, 1973)
Russell Taylor, John *The Second Wave* (Eyre Methuen, 1971)
Tynan, Kenneth *A View of the English Stage* (Paladin, 1975)

Specific Aspects

Anderson, Michael *Anger and Detachment: A Study of Arden, Osborne and Pinter* (Pitman, 1976)
Benjamin, Walter *Understanding Brecht* (New Left Books, 1977)
Brecht, Bertolt *Brecht on Theatre* translated by John Willett (Eyre Methuen, 1978)
Browne, Terry *Playwright's Theatre: The English Stage Company at the Royal Court* (Pitman, 1975)
Jackson, Tony (ed) *Learning Through Theatre* (Manchester, 1980)
Joseph, Stephen *Actor and Architect* (Manchester, 1964)
O'Toole, John *Theatre-in-Education* (Hodder and Stoughton, 1976)

Magazines and Journals

Gambit, The Performance Magazine, Performing Arts Journal (USA) Platform, Plays and Players, Primary Sources, Theatre Quarterly, Time Out, SCYPT Journal

Index

Figures in *italic* type refer to illustrations

Acknowledgements

The editor and publisher wish to thank all those who kindly supplied photographs for this book.

Alex Agor, 96, 97 (top)
Michael Bennett, 104
Bob Bird, 133
Birmingham Repertory Theatre, 174
Romano Cagnoni (Report, London), 11
Donald Cooper, 89
Coventry TIE Company, Belgrade Theatre, 81
Chris Davies, 111, 119, 159
Chris Davies (Report, London), 90
Peter Harrap (Report, London), 53, 67, 108
Barry Jones, 44
Mike Laye, 73, 103
Peggy Leder, 107, 125, 130
Liverpool Playhouse, 167 (right)
Local Studies Library, Nottinghamshire County Library, 168
Manchester Public Libraries, 167 (left)

Daniel Meadows, 100 (bottom)
Rod Morrison, 93, 148
Alastair Muir, 127, 140
Roger Perry, 21, 27, 54, 97 (bottom), 99, 100 (top), 155
Perspectives Theatre Company, Peterborough, 83
Jill Posener, 57
Christopher Schwartz, 41, 63, 179, 185
Laurie Sparham (International Freelance Library Ltd.) 161
Staffordshire Sentinel Newspapers, 171 (top)
John Sturrock (Report, London), 35, 39, 137
Kelvin Tilfourd, 71
Victoria Theatre, Stoke, 171 (bottom)
Andrew Wiard (Report, London), 143, 151, 176